Born in Finglas, North Dublin, in 1959, **Dermot Bolger** is one of Ireland's best-known writers. His thirteen novels include *The Journey Home*, *Father's Music*, *The Valparaiso Voyage*, *The Family on Paradise Pier*, *A Second Life*, *New Town Soul*, *Tanglewood* and *The Lonely Sea and Sky*. His first play, *The Lament for Arthur Cleary*, received the Samuel Beckett Award. His numerous other plays include *The Ballymun Trilogy*, which charts forty years of life in that Dublin suburb; a stage adaptation of James Joyce's *Ulysses*, which was staged by the Abbey Theatre in 2017; *Walking the Road*, about the life of Francis Ledwidge; *In High Germany*, which was filmed by RTÉ television, and its sequel – twenty years on – *The Parting Glass*. His first collection of poems, *The Habit of Flesh*, was published in 1980 and his tenth and most recent collection is *That Which is Suddenly Precious: New & Selected Poems 1975-2015*. As an eighteen-year-old factory hand in Finglas, Bolger founded Raven Arts Press, which he ran until its closure in 1992. He devised the best-selling collaborative novels, *Finbar's Hotel* and *Ladies Night at Finbar's Hotel*, and has edited numerous anthologies, including *The Picador Book of Contemporary Irish Fiction*. A former Writer Fellow at Trinity College, Dublin and Playwright in Association with the Abbey Theatre, Bolger writes for most of Ireland's leading newspapers and in 2012 was named Commentator of the Year at the National Newspapers of Ireland Journalism Awards.

www.dermotbolger.com

# By the Same Author

# Bang Bang
## and Other Dublin Monologues

# Bang Bang

## and Other Dublin Monologues

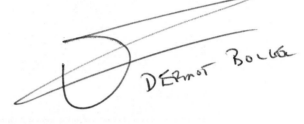

## Dermot Bolger

NEW ISLAND

BANG BANG AND OTHER DUBLIN MONOLOGUES
First published in 2017 by
New Island Books
16 Priory Hall Office Park
Stillorgan
County Dublin
Republic of Ireland
www.newisland.ie

In partnership with
Dublin's Culture Connects
Dublin City Council
3 Palace Street
Dublin 2
Republic of Ireland
www.dublinscultureconnects.ie

Print ISBN: 978-1-84840-658-2

Typeset by JVR Creative India
Cover design by Mariel Deegan

These monologues – *Bang Bang*, *The Messenger*, *Rope Knots* and *Waiting to be Found* – were commissioned by Dublin's Culture Connects as part of The National Neighbourhood: Press Play project 2016.

# Dublin's Culture Connects

Culture is central to human development and quality of life, and so Dublin's Culture Connects projects embed culture in the everyday life of the city. The programme builds engagement and connection through partnerships that are meaningful to the citizens. We are stronger together, and Dublin's Culture Connects is a catalyst, bringing different people together to have fun and develop empathy, understanding, and respect through culture.

Through one of our lead projects, The National Neighbourhood, we want every neighbourhood to know and own their city's cultural resources so we build cultural projects in community settings. We connect artists, groups and villages with libraries, museums and creative places to deepen their understanding of each other and themselves.

These monologues by Dermot Bolger were commissioned as part of Dublin's Culture Connects: The National Neighbourhood in 2016. A specfic project, called Press Play, was developed under the project management of axis Ballymun with artists and people in the North West Area of Dublin in partnership with the Abbey Theatre and the National Museum of Ireland and with Dublin City Council.

In Press Play, throughout the year, some ninety workshops were hosted by numerous artists in the local area, nineteen cultural tours or visits took place and a whole host of pop-up museums, culture clubs and events took place on the streets, in the libraries and in people's homes with hundreds of people locally.

The National Neighbouhood was in its pilot year in 2016 and is set to continue into the future and will evolve and re-imagine. As the conversations from yesterday continue today, we look forward to keeping the spirit of community, creativity and collaboration alive.

We would like to thank everyone who is connecting, engaging, creating and exploring with us.

*Iseult Byrne*
*Project Director, Dublin's Culture Connects*
*www.dublinscultureconnects.ie*

*With special thanks to the Press Play project partners:*

# Author's Note

Every street corner has its unique story. Every curved road in Finglas or Cabra, or indeed any suburb of any city across the globe, has not just one hidden history but a myriad of forgotten interlinked stories waiting to spill out from the façade of bricks and mortar, which is all that any casual passer-by ever sees.

Like many Dubliners who walk the streets of this, their native or adopted city, I am fascinated by how I am unable to walk past certain seemingly unremarkable spots without these places summoning up a rush of personal memories or stories that I overheard about the people who once lived there. But rather than make me any sort of expert on my native city, it merely reinforces just how little I truly know – or indeed how little anyone can truly know – about the interweaving tapestry of lives stretched back across generations which make up the human DNA of a city.

Therefore in 2016, when I walked into the coffee shop of the National Museum of Ireland, Collins Barracks, where I was Writer in Residence, to meet with Emma Connors – Arts Development Manager of axis Ballymun, who were project managing the 'Press Play' project as part of Dublin's Culture Connects: The National Neighbourhood – my reply was instantaneous when Emma asked if I wished to become involved.

I knew at once that I wanted to tell stories about certain people and places which had long fascinated me, and not just to try to tell these stories to an audience who might be unaware of them but to also try and fill in the missing gaps in these narratives in my own mind, to try and construct reimagined versions of the lives of people about whom I only knew scraps of information. All four monologues in this book stem from stories that I told Emma as we sat over our first coffee.

When I started Raven Arts Press in Finglas in the late 1970s I was hugely supported by two wonderful Cabra men: the local historian Bernard Neary and the songwriter Martin Sneyd, who had set up a Cabra Arts Group. They ran events in Cabra which I took part in. A mainstay of those events – which included local performers from all generations – was an elderly lady of enormous warmth and charm, the late Rose O'Driscoll. Rose's poems evoked the Cabra that her family had moved out to during the Second World War after the devastation caused by the Nazi bombs that fell on the North Strand. Many families from that part of Dublin needed to be transported out to homes and streets in Cabra that were just not ready for them. The story of how this community remade itself in Cabra after the North Strand tragedy always fascinated me. Many books have proved useful in fleshing out the links between Cabra and the North Strand bombings – from Bernard Neary's series of local histories (the most recent entitled *Dublin 7*), to Kevin C. Kearns' *The Bombing of Dublin's North Strand, 1941*. But the real inspiration for *The Messenger* goes back to the childhood stories Rose O'Driscoll told me at those small gatherings in Cabra thirty-five years ago. I hope I have done some justice to the families who made that journey.

I am sure that Rose O'Driscoll mentioned Bang Bang (Thomas Dudley) to me because any Dubliner I ever met who was a child in the 1940s, 1950s and 1960s retains vivid memories of this street character who jumped down from open-backed buses to instigate imaginary Wild West gun battles. In January 1981 when a tiny number of mourners gathered in the tiny Rosminian cemetery in Drumcondra, there were three names they might have carved onto the tombstone of this famous Dublin character whom they were burying.

Firstly they could have carved "Thomas Dudley", the name that he was born with in Inchicore in 1906, before being raised in a Cabra orphanage. But this name is unfamiliar to thousands of Dubliners who, for decades, found themselves caught up in mock shootouts with him, swept along by his anarchic and infectious humour. Secondly they could have inscribed the name he adopted after he lost his sight and began being cared for in Clonturk House – the Rosminian home for the blind in Drumcondra. Here, in his final years, the gunslinger humorously preferred to be addressed as "Lord Dudley the Devil".

Thirdly they could have inscribed the nickname "Bang Bang" by which he was known by every Dublin child with whom he engaged in imaginary shootouts during decades of skirmishes with outlaws and desperadoes who manifested themselves to him in the shape of bus conductors, passengers and passers-by during his decades as a constant presence on Dublin's streets. "Bang Bang" were the words he shouted – and were shouted back at him – whenever he opened fire with the huge key he carried in his pocket, which magically became transformed into a Colt pistol during moments when the whole street suspended disbelief and entered into his eccentric, fun-loving fantasy world.

In that fantasy world Dublin became Dodge City, Whitehall merged into Wyoming, Marino became Missouri and a Dublin bus could be transformed into a stagecoach, with his presence saving the passengers from being attacked by Sioux braves on horseback. But in 1981 none of these names were carved onto a tombstone because he never got one. While Bang Bang's life as a gunslinger was richly imaginative, in real life Thomas Dudley had few material possessions. Street characters appear from nowhere and disappear into nowhere. They become so much a part of the backdrop of our lives that we cease to notice them until one day we notice their absence. It is impossible to explain their role in the rich tapestry of Dublin life to new generations who never heard of Bang Bang or Johnny Forty-Coats or other characters who populated our streets, leading lives at once colourful and sad.

Behind his public gaiety Bang Bang's life was tough. Initially homeless after leaving that orphanage, he later had a small flat on Bridgefoot Street. His neighbours there, and in Mill Street in the Coombe (where he lived for many years), looked out for him as best they could, but in his later decades Dublin changed, with heroin addicts barging into his flat to shoot up. The Rosminian fathers sheltered him and buried him with dignity in their small cemetery. But he has continued to haunt Dubliners' imaginations, and indeed my own, which is why I told Emma his life story when we sat down to talk, and why I wrote the title monologue in this book. It is my attempt – as a creative writer and not an historian – to try and fill in the gaps in his life and make sense, in my own mind at least, of the great impulse to play which motivated him to roam Dublin's streets.

Nobody thought to offer Thomas Dudley a headstone until Daniel Lambert – who runs the Bang Bang Café in Phibsborough – organised a fundraising campaign to erect a memorial to mark the resting place of Dublin's most famous gunslinger. The exact location of Bang Bang's grave was known only to a dwindling handful of people, notably Joe Tyrrell, who – as cemetery caretaker – was involved in his burial in 1981 and carefully noted the unmarked spot. I felt hugely honoured when the actor Pat McGrath was asked to perform an extract from this monologue at Thomas Dudley's grave on August 28th 2017 when a small memorial plaque, engraved with a golden key, was unveiled by the Lord Mayor of Dublin, Mícheál Mac Donncha, with Joe Tyrrell again present, this time as part of a far larger crowd there to pay homage to this legendary Dublin street character.

If Bang Bang's story remains widely spoken of, this is in contrast to the story of John Bell of Finglas, shot at dawn in France in 1915 at the age of twenty. When I first encountered his name, many years ago while researching a play about Francis Ledwidge, the only wording I could find was three stark sentences: "Driver John Bell of Finglas, Dublin. Royal Field Artillery. Shot at dawn".

The intervening years have seen a long and finally successful attempt to restore the reputations of John Bell and twenty-seven other executed young Irishmen, spearheaded by the "Shot at Dawn" campaign. An intensive re-examination of each case by the Irish Department of Foreign Affairs embarrassed the British government into granting a belated pardon to these men. I notice that his listing with the Commonwealth Graves Commission now reads "In Memory of Driver John Bell, Royal Field Artillery who died on 25 April 1915. Son of John Bell, of Finglas, Co. Dublin. Remembered with Honour."

I am greatly indebted to Stephen Walker, who wove together the lost stories of Irish soldiers executed during the First World War in a superb book entitled *Forgotten Soldiers: The Irishmen Shot at Dawn*. In it Walker records how Irish government officials found that the officers who quickly issued such death sentences often had "little or no legal experience". There was a remarkable disparity about the treatment of Irish volunteers. Although soldiers from every nationality were tried for desertion and disobedience in that war, Irish volunteers were almost four times more likely to be sentenced to death than soldiers of other nationalities.

An official memo laid out the steps for their executions in exacting detail. Prisoners were stood upright, feet tied not more than twelve inches apart. Their hands were to either hang by their sides or be tied behind their back, with six inches of play between their bound hands and the post to which they were tied. In order to ensure that any straps used inflicted no permanent marks on prisoners, the War Office in London even helpfully provided a diagram.

The institutional prejudice about Irish volunteers started at the top of the British Army: an inbred suspicion that the Irish needed discipline and had to constantly be made an example of. In an era with no understanding of post-traumatic disorders, an era where boys suddenly found themselves amid the inhuman horror of no man's land, soldiers were often sentenced to death for going missing or simply becoming separated from their units amid the confusion. The vast majority of sentences were commuted, but where morale or discipline was weak, an execution was seen as an effective method of instilling backbone.

Stephen Walker quotes an ex-soldier, Leslie Bell, who recalled being marched for hours in 1917 to hear the news that two fellow Ulstermen, James Templeton and James McCracken, had been shot: "*There were great murmurs in the ranks at this statement. The colonel gave a yell: 'Order in the ranks, or I will have every sixth man shot!' Of course that kept everyone quiet… These two lads had been sacrificed to set an example to the rest of us. We never had the same respect for the officers when we found out that anyone could meet the same fate.*"

Many of the twenty-eight Irishmen who, like John Bell, were sentenced to death, had little education. Many were already traumatised by what they endured and had little means of defending themselves in a military court. Today Bernard McGeehan from Donegal would be regarded as having "special needs": in 1916 he was simply described in his trial as "a worthless soldier" and shot. Benjamin O'Connell from Wexford was unable to read or write. Sometimes they were secretly given morphine in their drinks on the night before their deaths, or in the case of the Ulsterman James Crozier, were simply got senselessly drunk so that he knew little about the ordeal.

I knew very few details about my fellow Finglasman John Bell, who died aged twenty. But many families of executed men simply received a curt postcard, often weeks or months later, which contained no expression of sympathy, explanations of their supposed crimes, or account of their court-martial. In the monologue *Rope Knots* I tried to create a life for this Finglasman written out of history, a rationale for how he found himself lost and scared in a war that possessed neither logic nor reason. I am greatly indebted to Christopher Lee for his very thorough and fine research into the riot by agricultural labourers that occurred in Finglas village during the 1913 Lockout, which culminated in the shooting of Patrick Daly. But as a playwright I am only speculating as to whether the real John Bell witnessed the shooting of this unarmed striker by Constable Barry.

My favourite spot when I was growing up in Finglas was the small graveyard and ruined church at the heart of Finglas village: a village divided in two by an intrusive dual carriageway when I was a child. The late Thomas (Dano) Lynch who lived in a small cottage beside the graveyard gates was always courteous and generous to me as a teenager when I would knock on his door to ask for the key so that I could sit beside the Nether Cross there. I am delighted to have the chance to retell the story of that cross, which was told to me when I was a child, and felt very honoured that members of the Lynch family were among the many local people who turned up in that graveyard to see Ali Dempsey give the first full performance of *Waiting to be Found* there, beautifully directed by Elizabeth Duffy, just two months before Thomas Lynch, the custodian of that cemetery, passed away.

The four stories here are only very tiny fragments salvaged from time and lost within the overall narrative of all the life stories of Dublin city. But, whether invented or reimagined, they are precious to me. I am deeply grateful to Iseult Byrne, Project Director of Dublin's Culture Connects; to Rowena Neville, Communications Director of Dublin's Culture Connects; and to Emma Connors, who, as I say, acted as coordinator for The

National Neighbourhood: Press Play project, and was very generous with her time and commitment.

I was blessed in being allowed to work with such wonderful performers in Pat McGrath, Clarabelle Murphy, Ali Dempsey and Martin Donnery and with such innovative directors as Mark O'Brien, Phil Kingston, Elizabeth Duffy and Andrea Ainsworth who all brought passion and great craft to the task of bringing these monologues to the stage.

A very special thanks to Lorraine Comer, Head of Education at the National Museum of Ireland, and all the staff at the National Museum of Ireland in Collins Barracks, who generously provided a room where these four monologues where written. My thanks also to everyone at the Abbey Theatre where these plays were first performed to a specially invited packed audience of people from Finglas, Cabra, Ballymun and Whitehall – many of whom had also participated in the huge range of events which formed part of the overall The National Neighbourhood: Press Play project.

I am grateful to members of the projects' Advisory Group who included Phil Kingston, The Abbey Theatre; Lorraine Comer, The National Museum of Ireland; and Aisling Murray, Dublin City Public Libraries and Archive; Sinead Connolly, City Arts Office, Mary Taylor, Aidan Maher and Larry Dooley, North West Area Office – all with Dublin City Council and Emma Connors of axis Ballymun and Iseult Byrne of Dublin's Culture Connects.

If I had a final wish for these monologues it is not just that they would be performed and enjoyed but that they might also inspire emerging writers and theatre practitioners to go on and reimagine, reinvent and retell those personal stories which they in turn hold close to their own hearts.

*Dermot Bolger*
*August 2017*

# Bang Bang

*Bang Bang* was first performed, in abridged form, on the stage of the Abbey Theatre, Dublin, on 22 February 2017 as part of the Dublin's Culture Connects: The National Neighbourhood Press Play Showcase. It was first performed in its entirety, by the same actor, in the Axis Art Centre, Ballymun, on 23 March 2017.

Performer:     Pat McGrath
Director:      Mark O'Brien

*For Marian Fitzpatrick and Tina Robinson,*
*both blessed with the gift and generosity to create the space where*
*art happens.*

*Lights come up on an old man, THOMAS DUDLEY, sitting in a nursing home armchair. Dressed untidily with ruffled hair, he raises his head sleepily as if woken from slumber. But as he peers intently at the audience his gaze gains such a level of manic animation that at times he struggles to keep up with his own flow of words.*

Don't think that, just because I've gone blind, I can't see you all out there gawking up at me, like I was a star on the silver screen. Have you never seen a gunslinger before or indeed a grand lord dolled up in all my finery? That's who I am now: Lord Dudley the Devil, to use my exact title. So don't you forget it or start mouthing that other moniker which used to be pinned to my chest like a sheriff's tin star.

I sense you all staring because I spent my life staring back at the likes of you gazing at me. But don't you draw on me just because my sharpshooting days are done. So slowly does it: drop your right hands, with your middle fingers shaped into the barrel of a Colt revolver; your thumb raised like its hammer and your pinky finger itching to pull the trigger. There ain't no more guns allowed in this here saloon. Even if there was, you still couldn't outdraw me, blind and all as I am. But, I'm telling you, I've hung up my holster since joining the haughty taughty aristocracy.

*He rises from the chair now so that he can begin to act out the action in the play.*

I even smell my own poshness these days, because hardly a day goes by without some injun squaw in a nurse's uniform traipsing into this ward, filled with blind complaining old men, to bathe me, privates and all, if you don't mind. They run a scratching rake through my untidy mop of hair, as if they think they can just comb away decades of tumbleweed and prairie dust. There's a fierce amount of cleanliness and posh grub too – oxtail soup and all – involved in becoming a pillar of the gentry. But my elevation to nobility has put a halt to my years of gunfights on street corners or in cinema queues where young fellows used to bite the dust in slow motion, hoping to impress an Angelica on their first date so that she wouldn't just give him a brush-off with the mitten. But I never just fought riff-raff and prairie rats, I enjoyed many a duel at ten paces with blue-stockinged toffs when they were vacating ace-high eating houses off Grafton Street: establishments that employed waiters whose noses get turned up at birth to make it easier for them to look down on a humble cowpoke like me who's simply trying to keep the peace in this lawless frontier town of Dublin.

And nor will you see me ever again swinging out of the pole on the rear platform of open-backed double decker buses so that I can pick off addled-headed outlaws like you scrawny lot, one by one, with thundering bullets fired from my trusty rusty key. But ask me nicely though and I'll tell you tales about all the gun battles fought between Wyoming and Whitehall. Like the time I was helping a number 19 stage coach to make the dangerous crossing through the narrow gorge of Dolphin's Barn Bridge and the bogman bus conductor who was riding sidekick starting mouthing at me:

*A jocular slightly mocking country accent:*

"Come on, Bang Bang," he shouts. "You're losing your touch; you're letting the last injun escape. Can you not see that young

Sioux brave scrambling back up onto his piebald? That fellow will ride bareback up the Canal to Inchicore to let Sitting Bull know that you're riding shotgun on my bus. Sitting Bull will have half the Sioux nation chasing after us on horseback by the time we get to Phibsborough in this poxy traffic. It's all right for a footloose desperado like you but the inspector in the Broadstone Garage will keep me there half the night filling in forms to explain why so many arrows are sticking out of the back of the bus, destroying the paintwork. The shop steward representing the cleaners will be wanting time and a half."

*Own voice*

I made no reply to that snapper-head's balderdash. You can't waste time conversing with bus conductors. Half of them are greenhorn bog trotters and the rest ignorant guttersnipes – especially the half-witted buckaroos who try to stick me up for the bus fare, when I merely ride on their back platforms as a hired gun for their own protection. Not that there aren't some decent conductors who'd hand you a sandwich from their lunch boxes if they think you look peckish. But you have other conductors who don't realise that bushwhackers and banditos are lying in wait on every second street corner in Dublin, with barrel boarders and triggermen loitering on every other one. Dodge City has nothing on Dublin city, and while no town in Missouri was safe when Jesse James and his gang were riding roughshod, at least the sheriffs there never had to contend with cyclists trying to plough into them every time they jumped down from the stagecoach in a hurry. I'd like to see how far the buses in Dublin would get without me on the rear platform to ward off cattle-rustling mutton punchers and saddle tramps. I mean, translate the words from the injun tongue and you'll find they even called Córas Iompair Éireann after me: Crusader Packing Iron. I never asked them to: I was embarrassed enough by how they named Sherriff Street in my honour.

So inanyway I hobbled my tongue that day when the number 19 bus trundled down through the Dolphin's Barn gorge. I gave the buck eejit conductor a conspiratorial grin with the few yellow nashers I have left as he gibbered on about Sitting Bull. Did he take me for a gobdaw or a Kildare man? Everyone knows that Sitting Bull and I parlayed this long time ago, smoking the peace pipe in his wigwag up beyond Inchicore, sitting cross-legged with nothing between us but companionable silence and the remnants of two singles and two smoked cod that Sitting Bull sent his favourite squaw out to Macari's chip shop to fetch in for us.

He must have been one dim-witted conductor to think that Sitting Bull would attack his bus with me on board. I was his passport to get safely but shag him because I was about to put my trusty rusty key back in its holster and jump sticks at the next stop, dodging them cyclist outriders, to whale away the afternoon with my amigos all along the South Circular Road. If that conductor ended up having to explain to his inspector up at the Broadstone depot why every pensioner who got on board at Rialto to go and do the Nine Fridays in Berkeley Street Church, all wound up being scalped by Sioux braves in a surprise attack at the Black Church, that was his problem and he'd have no right to drag my name into it.

*He gives a menacing glare at the audience.*

I'm talking about my other name before I rechristened myself Lord Dudley the Devil. And you needn't pretend that you don't know my name. There was a time when every lily-livered out-rider in Dublin felt a shiver of dread at the mere mention of it.

*He shapes his fingers like a gun and aims while singing the opening lines of "Bang Bang (My Baby Shot me Down)".*

They even wrote songs about me back then – swarms of children chanting my name whenever I appeared on the corner of Bannow Road where the Batchelors factory churns out tins of baked Mexican strawberries. Them children cheered because children love to play and what class of merciful God would find any harm in that, or wouldn't enjoy gazing down from heaven to watch the classic gun battles we fought out: me chasing those tenderfoot chislers up Carnlough Road before they circled their wagons and regrouped to let out great injun whoops as they tried to pin me down in the steep Broombridge canyon, that is separated from the gulf of Finglas only by the width of the Rio Grande.

Those were good days on the range before I lost the sight in my eyes. And even the greatest gun slinger must accept that you can't go on peering into the darkness of the O.K. Corral, unsure if your peashooter will pop the clogs of the dastardly McLaury brothers or if you might accidently shoot Marshal Wyatt Earp or give good Doc Holliday a chronic dose of lead poisoning.

When there's nothing left to see expect the old films still playing in your head, it's time to retire to the bunkhouse, chew tobacco and peaceably spit your last into a spittoon. My Tombstone was changing – they put electronic doors on buses for a start, so cowpokes could no longer just jump on and off. The new drivers didn't want to pow-wow like the conductors used to, though some would say, "Sit down at the back, Bang Bang, and take the weight off your feet: you're looking fierce shook these days." But I couldn't settle in them seats. Nothing feels more peculiar than sitting down on a bus where you can't be shooting passengers dead with your trusty rusty key and you need to ding-dell a bell for the driver to open the door before you ride off into the sunset.

But there were some days near the end when I was so dog tired that all I could do was sit on a seat and stare out the window like the other passengers. In my old gun slinging days I used to always wonder what in God's name people were all staring out at. I didn't much like the view when I saw it. Dublin as spied through a bus window wasn't the city I knew at all – there was no fun on them streets – no cowpokes or saddle tramps. It funkified me because the place looked grown-up and fierce drab. It probably suits them folk that once had a childhood but it didn't suit me, back then when I suddenly felt like the oldermost cowpoke who ever lived.

Just doing simple thing becomes a chore when you wake up to find that you've been ambushed by time and the light keeps slipping further away. I had my little bunkhouse in the Liberties, warm and snug – in summer at least – and dry too, except when it rained to beat the Dutch. Even during gully washer showers you could shift your bedroll around till you found a dry spot where the ceiling didn't leak. But towards the end I had no peace there because the roundup boss must have hired a whole new posse of rough ranch hands. They kept bunking in with me at the oddest hours, sticking bottles of stout in my fist and telling me to pay no heed to their hullabaloo, saying that because old Doc Holliday had gone too lame with gout to attend to them in person, they had no choice but to inject themselves with whatever medicine the good Doc had sent down to cure their rattlesnake bites.

St Patrick was a conman because, all of a slap, there was a plague of rattlesnakes infesting Bridgefoot Street and the Oliver Bond flats around then. No night passed without more bronco busters landing in on top of me, raving from snakebite and needing to inject themselves with the potions the Doc sent down. I enjoyed the bottles of stout they brought for me but those injections made them cowpokes so wild and scary that, if the Duke had been there, he'd have given them raw hide.

They were always leaving saddle bags in corners and warning me not to touch them before they'd scatter again, leaving me alone on my tod. But I'd managed fine on my tod for years, cooking up tins of Batchelors' baked Mexican strawberries, until one day the gas company glimmer man burst in and says:

*Concerned Dublin accent:*

"Jaysus, Bang Bang, I'm fierce sorry but I have to cut off your two ring cooker – the ancient thing is a death trap. Your whole flat is, with so many used needles scattered around it that junkies must be using your gaff as a shooting gallery. You need to mind who you let in, Bang Bang: there's young lads taking advantage of you. Do you know what I'm saying?"

*Own voice:*

I didn't know the hell what he was saying. There was no shooting happened in my bunkhouse because I'd have heard the shots and taken out my trusty rusty key to keep the peace. I cursed him for sticking his nose in because the following morning didn't a bunch of Culchie peelers arrive in smelling of cabbage with their hobnail boots and Templemore accents. They kept talking nonsense about thieved goods being stashed there and asking did I know that six stolen televisions were stacked in the corner. Of course I didn't know or I'd have tried to find a cowboy film on them.

The peelers took away the whole kit and caboodle and the young ranch hands weren't one bit pleased when they tuned up the next night, full of snakebites and jitters. One of them landed a few kicks at me and a Calamity Jane with him said to leave me alone: that I was only an unfortunate half-wit cretin. I wanted to say that I was the sheriff in this town, but I curled up and played dead till they saddled up and rode west.

I was rightly on my own after that, though I could still manage to eat my beans cold, like I'd done on many a dusty cattle drive through Wyoming. But finally my sight grew so bad that I'd be an hour struggling with a tin opener to open the smallest tin, with blood from my fingers soiling the sauce. Those days were tough because it's hard to venture out when you can't see where you're going, but harder still to sit indoors on my own when there's something about the darkness stealing away your sight that would make any soul lonesome.

I even missed those jittery cowpokes who'd been suffering from snakebite and must have surely ridden ahead to find a watering hole for the cattle. They'd left me behind to guard the campfire but I'd let it go out. Without the red glow and the smell of coffee brewing they couldn't find their way back. The nights got so black that all I had for company was my own voice shouting for them to come back for me. But I never knew that I'd been crying – night after night – until a necktie social lynching party of gringos broke down my door. I curled up in fear because I sensed where those gringos had ridden in from – they smelt like the folk who work in asylums.

And wouldn't you just know it – but the one time when I truly needed my trusty rusty Colt 45 key to blast them all into the bone orchard in Tombstone city, I couldn't find it. The blasted key had slipped from my pocket during my fumbling around on the floor. Damn and tarnation. All I could do was grab whatever jam-jar I'd been using to drink cold tea from, or to wee into, and fling the contents at them, shouting, "I'm not going back: you can keep your electric shock treatment – to hell with your cables and sparks." I was expecting rough handling and felt as jittery as a cat in a roomful of rocking chairs, but the dame in charge of the posse spoke up in a good nun's voice – the parlour nun voice and not the classroom-nun-with-a-cane voice. She asks, real formal, like a Texas Ranger:

*Nun's voice:*

"Are you Thomas Dudley?"

*Own voice:*

The kind way she spoke that name shook me. The problem with kindness is that it brings back memories of how the kind nuns always used to try to shield me from the harsh boss nun in the early days of me being bushwhacked and taken hostage as a tiny child in the big house with high walls in Cabra. I knew that Thomas Dudley still lived in that big house because he'd grown so sad there, when we both lived together, that I'd had to leave him behind in the bad box when I made my escape. Thomas and me were like identical twins, or even closer, like the Lone Ranger and his horse, Silver. But sometimes even twins need to separate, because I couldn't bear being in the bad box anymore. "You're not putting me back in the bad box," I told this nun dame. "I don't belong in no bad box."

*Nun's voice:*

"I'm not trying to put you in any box. I want to bring you to Clonturk House in Drumcondra – the big house where the Rosminians care for the blind."

*Own voice:*

"I'm going nowhere with you. You'll take me back to the big house in Cabra where Thomas Dudley is hiding and all the doors are kept locked."

*Nun's voice:*

"That orphanage is Cabra is long closed down. And the doors of Clonturk House are never locked. You can come and go as you please, once you learn how to use a white cane."

*Own voice:*

The smell in my bunkhouse must have been something fierce bad because I could sense the other gringos in the lynch party doing their darndest to hold their breath and not breathe in the foul air. I was cornered like General Custard at Little Bighorn, and, to be honest, I was relieved because it's lonesome in the dark when the campfire has burnt out. "Are those other cowpokes working up on this Clonturk ranch?" I asked. "The ones who left me here when they rode ahead to find the watering hole?"

*Nun's voice:*

"You'll find plenty of old pals up there."

*Own voice:*

"How do I know you won't lock the doors of the big house like before?" I sensed her bend down to pick up something from the floor.

*Nun's voice:*

"Haven't you got your famous Colt 45 key?" She pressed it into my quivering fingers. "This key you've been shooting people with for half a century. That key is so large it would open any door. Where did you get it from?"

*Own voice:*

I felt less scared with my trusty rusty key in my grasp. "I got a loan of it off a lad named Adolf Hitler – long before he started getting up to mischief. He gave it to me the time he was working as a waiter up in the Shelbourne Hotel. They had to let him go – hairs from his moustache kept getting in the soup. He told me it was the key to the cell in the sheriff's office in the Shelbourne. I tried to return it but those doormen in the Shelbourne lobby are not overly welcoming of a poor cowpoke unless he's waving a sack of gold nuggets that he's after panning on his small claim." The nun dame laughed.

*Nun's voice:*

"Where do you get your imagination from, Thomas Dudley?"

*Own voice:*

"I stole my imagination back. It's not a sin to play. And I don't like being called Thomas."

*Nun's voice:*

"Will we call you Bang Bang up in Clonturk House? Would you prefer that?"

*Own voice:*

I held my trusty rusty key tight one last time and then I slung it into my pocket. "That name won't do now that I've hung up my shooting iron. You'd best use my proper title from now on: The Right Honourable Your Worshippable Lord Dudley the Devil."

And that's how I came to spend my days up here in Clonturk House, drinking sugary tea and having a good spit when the mood takes me, because they can take away a cowboy's six-shooter but they can't take away his phlegm. If any visiting quack gets too annoying with his pills and stethoscopes and tormenting what's left of my poor eyes with his blazing lights and stinging drops … or if they ask too many questions about my wild days back in Deadwood, South Dakota … then my spit misses the spittoon and I hear it splat onto their neat polished black shoes. That settles their hash and tells them to go boil their shirt with all their questions about my past. I'm not keen on talking about the past. The past has its secrets and those secrets stay past.

*He peers blindly towards the audience.*

Will you lot ever be finished looking up here at Lord Dudley the Devil? It's like you've never seen the devil before.

*He sings.*

"There's some that says the devil is dead and buried in Killarney."

*Stops singing, more serious.*

That song is rubbish. I've seen the devil and he regularly visits that big house with high walls in Cabra. I don't care if this new dame nun claims that the orphanage is knocked down. I know it's still standing because Thomas Dudley is still locked in there, aged seven years old. He got put in the bad box by the boss gospel sharp, a six-foot-two sin-buster in a black cassock.

*He shivers as if still scared by the memory.*

I know I sinned there. I just didn't know that I would be committing a sin by laughing with another boy, happy to enjoy the fresh air as we walked across the orphanage yard to the chapel to learn all the what-not and can't-do rules so that our souls could be scrubbed clean enough to make our first communions. Up until that day us chislers had only ever been minded by nuns – mostly kind nuns with smiles and occasionally strict nuns with canes, but at least you always knew where you stood with a nun – out of lasso range was possible. But this communion business was such a serious conundrum that they needed to haul in one of the head honchos to learn us the bunkhouse rules. This was why the nuns handed us over to the biggest toad in the puddle, a vexed ramrod with his white collar stiff with starch and indignation.

As we crossed the yard in a big line, heading for the chapel for our don't do instructions, a boy in front of me glanced around and reached his hand down by his side. He drew first and I drew back, copying his gesture, not even knowing I was drawing a gun because I'd never seen a cowboy film. Indeed I'd never even seen a knife and fork in that place. All I knew of the world were the high walls of that house out in the Badlands of Cabra.

I don't remember having ever played any games at all before until this boy, who'd only arrived and didn't yet know the law, smiled and drew his pretend gun on me. So I drew back, unaware that the priest was walking behind us. This gossip-sharp saw us and drew his weapon too: only his weapon was a leather strap. We must have made him as mad as a hornet because his strap rained down across our legs and our backs for committing the sin of playing. That man's strap was doing its darndest to learn us about the holy joys of making our communion. Before that day I'd never stood out as a bad egg, but from then on I was marked down as a desperado every time that sin-busting gospel-sharp arrived to teach us how to properly love Christ. I had to learn some way to survive his onslaughts because the nuns were too cowed and outranked to prevent them. Finally I escaped by the simplest of tricks: I learnt to stop time. Every time his leather strap bore down on my head, I made it descend as slow as molasses in January until it was barely moving by the time it struck my skull because, by then, I was barely still there.

His beatings hardly hurt at all because I made my jail break from that Mexican fortress in the only way I could – by conjuring up an axe in my mind and chopping myself in two. It's a right dandy trick if you can do it. His strap might be leathering away at the cowing Thomas Dudley but I'd taken myself off in my mind to some other place which I couldn't rightly recognise yet. I just knew that if I managed the card trick of becoming someone else then I didn't have to always be the cretin, the moron, the dim-witted amadán simpleton named Thomas Dudley. Thomas Dudley could tear up Jake, sobbing and crying in the black box in the big house in Cabra whenever the gospel-sharp visited us with his hobnails, but I'd learnt how to skedaddle. I was galloping across the prairie and even if my mare was only skin and bones and barely more than buzzard bait – well that old nag still carried me free.

I kept making jail breaks in my mind every time the gospel-sharp obliged us with his company until – lo and behold – one morning doesn't the head nun, who was as ancient and ugly as a mud fence, tell me that it's my sixteenth birthday and I'm a big lad now. As a treat to make up for all my previous birthdays they'd forgotten about, she's opening the big gates for me. By fluke the gospel-sharp was on his way in, with his strap ready to teach the younger boys to love Christ. When he saw me leaving, he puts a half crown into my palm.

*Priest's voice:*

"On your way, Thomas," he says, "and I hope I've prepared you for the outside world. You'd be best advised to forget everything that happened behind these walls and find a rag and bone merchant who needs a strong pair of hands. If you ever see any boy from in here approach you on the street in the future then pretend you don't know him. You're a good simpleton and so remember to cause trouble to no one."

*Own voice:*

I felt like asking who could I cause trouble to when I knew no one? But I hoppled my lip and walked on through farmland and half-built housing estates until I stumbled upon the North Circular Road. By tarnation, what did I find there, only more cows than people? It was like stepping into a cattle drive across the Chisholm Trail through the injun territories of Oklahoma, only the North Circular Road had more cow shite than they have in the films and all the cowboys there were so saddle sore that they needed to walk in long black coats, waving hawthorn sticks and spouting cow instructions in Roscommon accents. "What the hell is this place I've landed in?" I asked one gringo. He gave a belly laugh.

*Roscommon accent:*

"It's called Cowtown, boy. Are you another of them poor bastards from the orphanage?"

*Own voice:*

"I'm no bastard," I said, "I'm just a cretin causing trouble to no man." I followed the cows who seemed to know where they were going, making enough hullabaloo to waken the dead. Down we went: the cowpokes waving sticks and me causing no trouble till we reached the crossroads at Phibsborough. I swung to the left because I could no longer bear the roars of the frightened cows. I paused for breath and, when I looked up, what did I find myself outside of only some peculiar class of palace: shining red brick and chiselled gold letters that spelt out The Bohemian Cinema. Gleaming steps led up to a lobby where an elderly dame sat behind a grille. I was so mesmerised that I walked up them steps, meaning to cause no trouble to anyone. I'd have run for blue murder if the dame had said boo, but instead she looks up from reading her a shiny American magazine – I think it was American because all the photos were of film stars and not nuns – and she says:

*Kindly Dublin accent:*

"Are you going inside, love? It's a cowboy one today. Do you want the cheap seats?"

*Own voice:*

I handed her my half crown and she handed me back a clatter of tuppences and pennies. Then it was up more steps, like I was entering the belly of a whale. This was no flea-trap joint, but a high-falutin' establishment as top notch as cream gravy. I thought the money I'd paid in was just to be allowed sit surrounded by such plushness, with carpets thicker than a Mississippi swamp and shapes of naked angels carved out of plaster on the ceiling. I didn't rightly even know what a film was until the joint went dark and this cranky looking German walked out and began to play his piano. Suddenly the screen lit up and – Mother of the Devine Jesus – didn't I suddenly spy myself up there on the screen, in that other life which I had been living when I used to jailbreak out in my mind whenever Thomas Dudley was being beaten in the bad box. All of a slap I had just found the other half of myself and it was riding free out there on the wild frontier where I belonged.

Until that day I'd never had a proper name for the place I used to go when splitting myself in two to escape from the gospel-sharp and let poor Thomas Dudley take the beatings for the both of us. But it seems that I'd been slipping off to the Bohemian Cinema, without even knowing that the place existed, to ride with amigos in a silvery world where there was no one to call it a sin when we drew our guns and shot and hollered and played dead.

And that's what I did when the film ended. I crawled under the row of seats, lying as still as if I had ten Cherokee arrows stuck in me. I didn't know what might possibly happen next in such a magical palace: I just knew that I felt at home at last. After a while a new posse of gringos trooped in and I thought they had come to look for me. But instead the lights went down and the cranky German banged the same notes from his piano again as my real world flashed back up on the screen: the whole story starting from scratch again. This time I could see that I was riding no buzzard bait, but a white horse that reared up on his hind legs every time the German hit a high note. That horse had one great ear for music, but he never threw me from my saddle because his responsibility was to keep me safe and my responsibility was to keep the peace in that tumbleweed town where card sharks in the saloon hid aces up sleeves and ranch hands snored in their bunks, stociously stupefied after passing around bottles of Sheepherder's delight.

I couldn't rightly tell you how often I lived out my life inside the film that day, hiding under the seats between every show until in the end even the cranky German got sick of exercising his fingers and headed of home for his tea. I'd have bunked down there for the night if a tenderfoot hadn't found me when he was clearing up. He was barely older than me but wore a braided uniform as grand as any general in the Confederate Army.

*Young Dublin accent:*

"You'll have to head, pal," he says. "We're closing the flick-house."

*Own voice:*

He looked at me then and winked, pulling a mean face like a braggart with too much mustard as he reached one hand down by his side. I feared I was for the chop and he'd pull out a leather strap. Instead his hand came back up in the shape of an imaginary gun.

*Young Dublin accent:*

"Bang bang," he shouted, "bang bang, you're brown bread, pal."

*Own voice:*

Quick as a flash I drew my own pistol, like I'd done that time when I was seven. But this time no sin-busting gospel-sharp was going to stop me playing. I shouted "Bang bang," so loud that I was afeared they'd hear me back in the orphanage, which was only two whoops and a holler away. The tenderfoot fell in slow motion and played dead on the plush carpet. It was the funniest sight I'd ever seen and the bestestmost ever feeling. I looked up at the plaster angels on the ceiling, fearful that God would strike me dead for this sin of playing but it felt as if God himself was laughing, not at me but with me. The tenderfoot laughed too, rising from the floor.

*Young Dublin accent:*

"You're a gas ticket," he said. "Now will you get the feck out so I can lock up?"

*Own voice:*

There was no one left in the lobby, no one on the shiny steps, the front door half closed over with a big key stuck in it. The tenderfoot was still inside, sweeping up. God forgive me because I'm no nibbler and I never stole nothing from no one before or since, but on that night I stole the big key from the Bohemian Cinema door because if that picture palace was magic, then surely the key to it must have magic too.

I hightailed it away at full chisel then, with no idea where it was safe to dodge down for the night. When I reached Dorset Street two young lads were holding up a street corner that must have needed supporting. I aimed my new key at them and shouted, "Bang bang, you're dead." And the key really

41

had magic because one of them laughed and fell down dead. I looked up at the sky but God didn't want to strike me dead for the sin of wanting to play. Then the realisation came to me that the sin-busting gospel-sharp in the black cassock in the bad lands of Cabra had not been a man of God at all, but must surely have been the devil.

During these past sixty years I've never ventured further into Cabra than the streets around the Batchelors factory, just in case the Devil is still waiting for me in the big house further up the road. But during all them years the devil was never able to stop me playing on buses and on street corners where strangers who saw me would shout "Bang Bang" before I'd even drawn my trusty rusty key. No man ever outdrew me. I shot the outlaws dead and kept the streets safe for folk to live and play on. A few ignorant folk have called me cracked and I got my share of kickings, but every frontier town has lunk-headed dumbbells. And what are a few cuts and bruises and busted ribs – and indeed what is being hungry and cold itself – to knowing that the devil was wrong and that folk in this here town want to play my game.

*He reverently removes an old large rusted key from his pockets and cradles it in his palm.*

Every shootout made me stronger and even though I've lost my sight I've kept hold of this trusty rusty key, because I know that this darkness I'm sitting here in isn't the end of the last reel. There's a wheeze in my chest and it's only a matter of time before this darkness deepens to the blackest pitch. I reckon I'll probably find this dying business pretty damn scary but – all of a flash as I struggle for my last breath – I'll hear the whirl of a projector and the silvery screen of the Bohemian Cinema will light up my eyes again.

This time I won't be afeared to step out from the cheap seats and walk up the aisle with a gunslinger's gait. I'll step right up to touch that screen and then I'll step through it and find myself flinging open the wooden swing doors into the saloon in Dodge City. He'll be sitting in there – the boss gospel-sharp from Cabra in his black cassock, playing poker for the soul of Thomas Dudley with Doc Holliday and the Duke and Billy the Kid. The Doc and the Duke and Billy will look down at the same time and step away from the table when they finally spy his cloven hoof. Then it will just be me and him, but this time I won't be scared of him because I've stolen his name like he once stole mine. I'll say, real slow, "My name is Lord Dudley the Devil: now reach for your gun and draw." The gospel-sharp will have four aces in his hand and a joker up his sleeve, but I'll be ready because I've been practicing for this shootout for sixty years. He'll make a sly move for the Derringer pocket pistol concealed up his other sleeve and I'll let him think he has me, for the half second it takes him to draw out his sneaky weapon.

*THOMAS DUDLEY raises the old key like a gun, aimed directly at the audience.*

Then I'll raise my trusty rusty Colt 45 and one last time I'll say the words I'm famous for: "Bang, bang, you're dead!"

*Lights fade.*

# The Messenger

The *Messenger* was first performed, in abridged form, on the stage of the Abbey Theatre, Dublin, on 22 February 2017 as part of the Dublin's Culture Connects: The National Neighbourhood Press Play Showcase, and in the National Museum of Ireland at Collins Barracks, on 2 March 2017.

Performer:    Clarabelle Murphy
Director:     Phil Kingston

*For Helen Bradley & in memory of Rose O'Driscoll.*

*MARGARET, a sixteen-year-old girl in a 1940s frock with a cardigan over her shoulder stands hesitantly centre stage and takes a few cautious steps forward before she stops and peers around. There is a minimal stage setting but from her words we gradually glean that she is standing on a half-built street corner where Dingle Road meets Fassaugh Avenue in the working-class suburb of Cabra in North Dublin. It is a dark and bitterly cold evening in late autumn, 1941. From her words and gestures we slowly gain a sense that although some of the terraces of Dublin Corporation houses on this estate are finished and occupied, many other terraces nearby remain only half completed, so that her immediate surroundings possess the atmosphere of a building site as much as a settled residential area. She glances down at the copy of the* Sacred Heart Messenger Magazine *which she holds in her hands – a religious magazine whose cover is always printed in a garish red – before her eyes settle on the audience as she begins to speak in a low, confiding voice:*

This is the one good thing to come out of it all, according to Da anyhow: my renewed piety and devotion to God. Not that I didn't believe in God before all this, but until last Wednesday I'd never asked Da if I could have his copy of *The Sacred Heart Messenger*, after he'd read it from cover to cover and was about to tear it up to help light the fire. (*She displays the cover.*) You know the Holy Josephine religious magazine, don't you? The best read devotional magazine in Ireland and the most red too, because they always print its front cover in gorgeous red ink. Even now, in the midst of Mr. Hitler's war when everything is rationed, from tea to tobacco, no government would dare deny the Jesuits their ration of red ink to print the Messenger.

I can't tell you too much about the pious articles inside it, to be honest, because I've never actually opened the magazine. I just took it out here with me last Wednesday – which was the first evening when I stepped out from our new home on Dingle Road into the freezing cold – though God knows the house isn't much warmer inside. And I've carried this same magazine with me on each of the past six evenings since then when I've carefully manoeuvred my way through the darkness to this spot where our half-built road ends, avoiding potholes and broken footpaths until I come to a halt at this black expanse of mud where folk claim that one day there's going to be a row of shops built across the road here and a new church and God knows whatnot.

God knows is right: you never know what God is going to send you, or where he's going to send you. Those distant lights to my right are Dublin city. Standing here where Dingle Road begins, I can see the beckoning city that was once our home and see also the terrible empty darkness in between that separates us from Dublin city with its dance halls and cinemas and lit shop windows where you can pause and gaze in the evenings.

They say that one day this dark expanse will be jam-packed with new streets and houses, but one day isn't now. I can only live in the here and now, and right now I'm a sixteen-year-old girl with forty minutes of freedom before Da stops fretting about Ma's morose silence for long enough to send my kid brother Jamie out here to scour the darkness for me.

The only thing lit up between here and Dublin is the first cluster of street lights that the Corpo have switched on, at the hump of the railway bridge on Fassaugh Avenue. Every girl old enough to flesh out a skirt is gathered over there by the looks of it, swarming like moths to a flame to that halo of electric light. Or at least those of us girls who are allowed out in the wilderness of Cabra, littered with sawn-off pavements where you'll never know if you'll step into a massive puddle where the Corporation workmen ran out of tarmac for the new roads they're frantically trying to finish.

I know exactly where there's such a puddle because, for these past six nights, I've stood here in this darkness, unable to bring myself to walk the two hundred yards up to that lit railway bridge on Fassaugh Avenue. It's like I'm frozen here between the life I've needed to leave behind and this new life that I'm not ready for yet. But tonight I'm going to find the courage to move; tonight I'll rip the front cover right off this *Sacred Heart Messenger* and use the inside pages for something to kneel on. We've all heard so many prayers said by so many priests over these past months that if anyone passes by in this darkness they'll probably just think that I'm kneeling here to pray too.

*She tears the cover from the magazine, and uses the inside pages to kneel on as she dips the cover into an imaginary puddle on the stage and looks up.*

But I'm not praying. I'm soaking the cover of the Messenger in this puddle until it is wringing wet and then I'm going to rub it into my cheeks because, under the street lights at that railway bridge, the red ink will easily get mistaken for the finest rouge you could buy in any posh makeup shop on Grafton Street.

*Still kneeling, she begins to rub the cover against her cheeks.*

The local yokels in this wild west of Cabra can call us North Strand girls anything they like, but they can never say that we're not sophisticated. I'm no country bumpkin like the big-hipped muck savages out here. I've already spent an hour up in my bedroom, warning Jamie that I'd burst him if he came in while I was drawing the seams of nylon stockings with a sharp pencil down the back of my legs, doing it so painstakingly that you'd swear I was wearing real nylons. I look so plush now that you'd mistake me for a gal waiting for an American GI, like Tyrone Power or Humphrey Bogart, instead of a mere shop girl who's walking out with Alfie O'Connor from North William Street.

That's a lie in two ways because since last Wednesday he's been Alfie O'Connor from Carnlough Road in Cabra – after his unruly tribe of eight brothers and four unwashed sisters all had to move into the new house that the Corporation have given them, which is so small they must sleep standing up in it. And it's a lie in a second way because Alfie and I are not exactly walking out together yet, on account of the fact that the stupid lump of an amadán hasn't actually asked me out on a date yet despite the fact I know full well how much he fancies the pantaloons off me.

I mean it's not my fault that the amadán simply began to fancy Grace even more. Well, he can forget thinking about her. I'll soon have him forgetting about Grace because I'm not making a holy eejit of myself out here, rubbing a magazine cover into my cheeks, to still play second fiddle to some …

*A pause as she rises.*

Alfie is so thick that he'll probably think real nylons are blue because that's the colour that my legs are turning in this biting cold. If Da could see how I've used safety pins to hitch up the hem of my skirt by six inches he'd probably lock me up into the new bedroom that at least is finally all mine. A bit of privacy at last because who'd want to always be sharing a bed with an annoying titch of a baby sister: all sharp elbow and twisting and growing taller in her sleep until, one morning all of a slap, she wakes up a good inch taller than me.

The sheer cheek of it: to be a year younger and nothing much to look at and then, overnight to suddenly not just be taller and more willowy in parts, but … well, let's just say that it's one thing to grow upwards, but it's nothing short of indecent and unfair for a younger sister to start expanding outwards as well, with strategic bits of her anatomy becoming so pert and pointy that they could take the eye clean out of a fellow's head. Or at least they could certainly catch a fellow's eye if he was as dim-witted as Alfie O'Connor, who – if he had any class or cop-on – would have kept his focus on a girl a year older and far more sophisticated.

But there's nothing worse for any fellow than giving them choice or free will. Give a fellow a choice and it's a racing certainty that he'll make the wrong bloody choice. So I'll tell you one thing, the girls hanging around that railway bridge tonight had better not give Alfie O'Connor too much choice, with their adoring cow's eyes, or I'll show them the true meaning of sharp elbows. Aye, and pinches in places that fellows like Alfie haven't even learnt to dream about. I've earned the right to walk out with Alife O'Connor as his mot and that right did not come cheap.

Some of our old North Strand neighbours who've moved up here to Cabra seem to be afraid of me or at least they don't know what to say to me. They're afraid of saying the wrong thing, as if there could be a right thing to say, as if there is anything right in this damnable cursed world. Well there isn't, and I feel like telling that to the next priest who pats my knee and natters on about God's will. The priests can try to make sense of it with their comforting words, just like the politicians tried to do with their grand speechifying, after they trooped out to be photographed with long faces and big overcoats, posing beside the smoldering pits where our homes used to be.

But I don't have any words. All I have is a pain burning me up inside that makes the biting wind blowing about my bare legs out here in this wilderness feel like nothing. Who wouldn't feel cold out in Cabra? The plasterer who was still skimming my bedroom wall looked at us as if we had ten heads when the Corpo dumped us here by truck last week with just a few donated horsehair mattresses and whatever few sticks of furniture we could salvage from our old house.

"Sure this house is just not ready for yiz," he said. "It will be months before these walls dry out. You must be daft."

He stopped then, all apologetic. "I spoke out of turn," he said. "You're not mad, you're desperate and I'm desperately sorry for you. Blast Herr Hitler anyway. Every carpenter and bricklayer has been working around the clock. We hadn't expected families to move in for another six months." He looked at my mother. "Still and all, it's a lovely house, Missus, and you'll turn it into a grand home. But I just wouldn't light a fire in the grate for another few months. If you do, the cinderblock is so damp still that the chimney is bound to crack."

And then he was gone – a nice man and the last workman we saw. We sat there for an hour on any wooden boxes or chairs we could find to sit on. We said nothing because these days we haven't got much left to say anymore as a family. Everything has been said; we needed to say those same words a thousand times to old neighbours – now ex-neighbours – to people from Summerhill that we barely knew and day-tripping gawkers from foreign parts like Glasnevin whom we didn't know at all and were just down for a look. I've listened to floods of words and yet none of them can properly describe what we endured on the Whit Weekend.

Me and Grace were already in bed that night – exchanging niggly elbows and sharp whispers as we quarrelled about all the attention Alfie O'Connor had started to pay to her and her pointy brassiere: attention he used to pay to me. Naturally we heard the planes circling overhead because they came in so low. But we paid them little heed because Nazi planes often fly past on their way to bomb cities in England. The war going on in Europe wasn't real to us, but Alfie O'Connor was real. That's why the two explosions just at midnight were such a shock. Had the pilot lost his way or lost his wits? The bombs were close but not too close: one at the corner of the North Circular Road and the next one, a few seconds later, in Summerhill. There was damage done all right; some families trapped under rubble – but, God forgive me, there was great comfort when we heard the third bomb explode a few minutes later because it sounded so far off and muffled. It blew a big crater up in the Phoenix Park where the only harm it did was to startle the elephant in Dublin Zoo who broke out of his enclosure to scatter the ducks on the lake by splashing his way down there because he felt safer in the water.

Still the commotion got the whole street up, with me and Grace racing downstairs in our dressing gowns. Nobody knew what was happening, but isn't it funny how males think the same – whether they be elephants or dockers – because the first instinct of Matty Finnegan, who lived three doors down from us, was to head straight for the drink too. We could hear him trying to batter down the door of McCormack's pub with his fists, shouting: "The Nazis are attacking: for the love of Christ, let me in, man: I need a ball of malt and a chaser."

Everyone was shocked, especially when a gang of young scuts came running down the length of the North Strand to tell us all how two houses had toppled over in Summerhill with fire brigade crews racing towards them. Me and Grace wanted to race up and see too, but Da said we were going nowhere, especially not dressed like that. Then the funny thing was, how after the first giddy rush of talk, everyone went dead quiet. It was such a peaceful night you could hear a pin drop. But we weren't listening for a pin. We were listening for any noise of returning planes.

Surely the Nazis must have realised their mistake at having bombed a neutral city and flown away. But gradually we heard the noise of one solitary pilot who seemed to be circling back towards us, as if he copped on to the error of his ways and needed to see with his own eyes how he had screwed up. I mean, how could anyone mistake Dublin for a blacked-out city like Liverpool when all the North Strand was lit up and the pilot could literally see us staring up at him in bafflement?

By this time the sky had become like a fairground attraction because the Irish army's air defences were shining huge beams of light upwards to crisscross the sky and they even fired off a clatter of harmless anti-aircraft shells to let the German eejit know that he was circling over the wrong city and should bugger off home. But the fellow just kept circling back over us, causing some women to panic and drag their children off to Charleville Mall Library because the caretaker there had opened the doors and was letting people take shelter in its basement. Ma asked Da if we should shelter down there too and Da said, "Shelter from what? Sure all the excitement is over."

He was right too. Or at least he was right for the bones of another hour and a half. Me and Grace were packed off back to bed, with the pair of us whispering to each other about what Summerhill must look like. But soon we drifted back to bickering about Alfie O'Connor again because even though that solitary plane remained up there circling us … it still felt unbelievably distant, with Hitler's war in Europe having nothing to do with us. We lived in our own little tightknit world down in the North Strand. Not that we didn't welcome strangers in from the east: Francie McCarthy next door had married a stranger from the East Wall and we all made her welcome, no bother.

I heard one o'clock strike on the clock above Corcoran's shop and then it struck half one and I told Grace that if the pilot hadn't finished his clowning around when Corcoran's clock struck two I was going down again out of curiosity, because even through the curtains we could see the great beams of light still being directed up into the sky to warn him to feck off home with himself.

When the clock struck two I nudged Grace and whispered if she wanted to come down for a gawk. But she was still in a huff after our row about Alfie O'Connor. "To hell with you then," I said, "I shouldn't need to share a bed with a titch like you: one day I'll have my own room."

I was worried that Da might be cross at me for getting up again, but he was standing in the same spot on the street, only now he was holding young Jamie's hand. Jamie was both sleepy and excited. Da looked as if one part of him was scared and the other half couldn't tell why.

I barely had time to say anything to Da because at five minutes past two the pilot dropped his bomb, like he'd spent all of that time eyeing up the perfect spot to give himself the chance to slaughter as many folk as possible. The screech of the bomb falling would stop your heart. There was the brightest flash and then a blast of scorching hot air like when you open an oven door. Only this blast was strong enough to knock over me and Da and Jamie and blow us thirty yards down the street and under the wheels of a parked lorry. Luckily for us the lorry didn't topple over because, while we were battered and bruised and cut, the weight of the lorry saved us from worse.

Thank Christ that during those seconds all I could see was a blocked view from underneath the truck because it felt as if the whole North Strand was being pushed outwards to greet me.

Whole walls toppled over, with big steel street lamps ripped clean out of the pavements like skittles. I saw Mr. McGrath come flying through his bedroom window in his nightshirt with startled eyes as if he couldn't believe that he'd been thrown across his room. Half his bedroom furniture came out the window after him and then the brass bed itself, not through the window but through the wall as if the wall was only made of paper and there was such heat that his mattress burst into flames in mid-air.

God forgive me, but I didn't care about Mr. McGrath just then or about the forty poor other souls who were losing their lives in our crumpled warren of small streets and cottages. I only cared about Grace and Ma and I knew that Da was the same. Because even though it felt like the blast had sucked every ounce of strength from our bodies, we somehow found the willpower to stagger up and out into that bedlam, with people screaming and fires breaking out everywhere. We both ran towards our front door that was half caved in, with Jamie staggering behind us. My face was cut from flying glass but I could feel nothing except fear. We reached whatever remained of our house, though we could barely make out anything amid the smoke and dust until another big spurt of flame arose across the street and let me glimpse our bedroom window where surely to God Grace could hear me calling her name.

It took days to locate some of our neighbours: their relatives digging and the army digging and so many gawkers arriving to offer their help that the Gardaí had to tell them to clear off because they were only getting in the way. There were children buried alive under heaps of rubble and stone, with their fathers and uncles desperate to find them and yet praying that they wouldn't be found – or at least not found dead. But they kept finding the dead in the oddest places: a corpse discovered four days later blown up onto the roof of the cinema, and fragments of bodies found hither and thither, with poor ARP wardens needing to try and piece them together.

The funny thing about Grace is that there was barely a scratch on her. The bedclothes were black with dust and smoke and her skin was blackened too, but you swear that she was asleep, except for the angle of her neck after having been thrown from our bed to collide with the wall. If she had only come down those stairs with me she'd still be alive. She would have come down too, if Alfie O'Connor hadn't started making eyes at her a few weeks before, with his buzz cut hair slicked back with Brylcreem. Because when we weren't fighting about him or some boy, we were the bestest of best friends and, sure, what is a sister for only to fight with and then make up afterwards and to share secrets with that you'd never tell another living soul.

You could ask Ma to tell you just how close me and Grace were, except that you can't really ask Ma anything about Grace. It was the kitchen table that saved Ma. The noise of the people out on the street, gawking up at the plane, had woken her and she'd gone down for a glass of water. It took five hours to dig her out – five hours that she spent with hordes of startled cockroaches crawling across her body; cockroaches scattering out from their nests in the clinker walls that were only made from horse hair and cinders of old coal.

When they found Ma, her voice was barely more than a whisper: hoarse and cracked from calling out our names during those hours breathing in dust and smoke. On Whit Weekend, 1941, she came downstairs as a good-looking woman to get a glass of water and when they lifted her, legs first, from the ruins of our kitchen, she was a grey haired old woman.

In the weeks after the bombing we were allowed to set up camp in Buckingham Street Fire Station. The man from the housing section in the Corporation thought that Ma must be my grandmother when he breezed in there to announce that we'd been given an emergency new house in Cabra. His voice had the same razzmatazz as if telling us that we'd won a prize in the Irish Hospitals Sweepstakes. And I could see him checking his list of names discreetly, baffled by who this old grey-haired woman was who kept staring blankly at him.

It's not that we don't know anyone up here in Cabra. The Farrells from North Clarence Street are now living on Dunmanus Road and the Kennedys are two doors up from us. But knowing people here doesn't make Cabra feel like home. And it always seems to be cold out here in the country where Da needs to queue in the muck for a single decker bus before dawn to get him to his work. Every evening he walks home because we have to save money where we can. I walk everywhere even into the draper in Summerhill who kept me on as his shop girl despite the fact that he could have got someone who lives far closer. And when I hand up my wages to Ma she gives me the same blank stare that she would now give if she opened an envelope from some relative in America and a thousand dollar bill fell out.

Nothing means anything to her anymore. She has a fear of insects and the look of a woman who'll never feel warm again. That's why she said to Da, on our first night in Cabra – and us barely two hours in the house – "Will you for God's sake light a fire, Johnny, or we'll freeze to death in this Godforsaken back of beyond where Hitler and the Corporation have landed us."

And damp plaster or no damp plaster, Daddy knew better than to argue in case she disappeared into one of her new silences that can last for days. So he sent me and Jamie out into the starlight, scrambling around half-built houses looking for any scrap of firewood. I didn't know whether to laugh or cry when we could barely find a spare piece of wood, because back in the North Strand now you can't move for falling over the ruins of people's homes that are now only fit for firewood. But when we brought back whatever few twigs we could find, Da had an *Evening Herald* scrunched up into knots that he could set alight to get the twigs going. He was about to tear up *The Sacred Heart Messenger* too, to help kindle the fire when I said: "Daddy, can I have the *Messenger*? I'd like to keep it."

"Well, that's the one good thing to come out of it all," Da said. "As long as you have your faith you are never lost, even though you have nothing else."

I have something else. I have fake rouge for my face and pencil marks down my legs as good as any pair of nylons. It's cold out here on this muddy corner where one day they say shops will be built. But I'm not just cold outside: there has been a chill inside me like ice since we found Grace with her neck broken.

But I also know there's surely a fire burning away somewhere deep inside me as well, because even in my sleep I smell smoke, and no matter how hard I scrub my clothes smoke seems to have seeped into every dress I could retrieve and every fold of my flesh. I can see the lights of Dublin a long way off. The first cluster of street lights at the railway bridge on Fassaugh Avenue are two hundred yards away but I can make out Alfie O'Connor leaning against the bridge there, chatting to some corner boys and a clatter of Carnlough Road floozies that are all beef to the heel like Mullingar heifers.

For these past six nights I've walked this far and been unable to go further. It's as if I'm trapped in this spot by the weight of mourning. But this evening I'm going to break free of that weight. I'm coming for you, Alfie O'Connor, you big witless eejit, and when I get a grip of you I'm going to stop feeling that there's only ice inside me. Tonight I'm starting to make a new life in this place and, even though you don't know it yet, I'm making that life with you.

Because, whatever it takes, I'm going to make you get over your mooching about Grace and make a move on me. I'll lure you away from the lights on that bridge and, when I do, I'll scorch the lips off you. There's so much smoke and flames trapped inside me that I have hotter lips than Hedy Lamarr or Dorothy Lamour or any of them Hollywood stars whose chests are always covered over in black paint when the ushers stick up film posters outside the Savoy Cinema.

I'm going to scorch you with such fire that you won't know what hit you and I'll let your hands stray just far enough to fully get your attention, because if you'd only given me your full attention in the first place then none of this would have happened. Grace would have come downstairs to stand with me out on the street, looking up as if that plane was some class of fairground attraction.

And on every date we have I will let your hand stray that quarter inch further – but no further – until you're driven so demented with desire by this fire inside me that you'll press a wedding ring on my finger and take me out of my parents' new house that's haunted by the dead. And we'll make a new life together – here in Dublin or more likely by having to take the boat train to England. I'll be a good and dutiful wife too and serve you up dinners and children, but you'll feel the sharp end of my tongue also on some evenings when these memories swell up and then you won't know what hit you. You'll be sitting in your chair looking up at me, all wounded eyes, saying "What did I do wrong?" And I'll never tell you until the day I die, you big thick eejit, because there are some secrets that stay secrets forever between sisters.

*Lights go down as she strides away.*

# Rope Knots

## A Finglas Life Reclaimed

*Rope Knots* was first performed, in abridged form, on the stage of the Abbey Theatre, Dublin, on 22 February 2017 as part of the Dublin's Culture Connects: The National Neighbourhood Press Play Showcase.

Performer:      Martin Donnery
Director:       Andrea Ainsworth

*For John Grundy, an essential, dissenting and illuminating voice within the Finglas community for many decades.*

*Lights come up on twenty-year-old JOHN BELL. Wearing a First World War British Army uniform, he stands with his hands joined behind his back. Initially there is no sinister indication within this stance, which merely gives him a relaxed appearance of casualness. He shrugs wryly.*

There's naught you can teach me about rope knots. Running bowlines and anchor hitches. That's one thing about growing up next door to an old sailor in Finglas. Jamsey Fagan taught me every knot by the age of seven. There wasn't nothing he couldn't do with a length of rope.

*Old man's voice:*

"Fetch my great coat and place it over my fingers, young John Bell," he'd say, sitting on the step outside his cabin. "Not many men can tie a soft shackle with their hands covered."

*His own voice:*

When I'd take his coat away again he'd have tied a perfect shackle knot and – like the soft daft eejit that I was then – I'd be awe-struck and too young to grasp how it didn't matter to Jamsey if he had ten coats covering his fingers because the old lad couldn't see what he was doing anyway – having gone blind as a bat. That's why Jamsey wound up living back in his brother's cottage: when sea captains realised that he couldn't do seafaring work no longer and simply walking down a rickety gangplank for him was as dangerous as a high-wire music hall act. But Jamsey still seemed to have eyes in the back of his head whenever he sent me off with a thrupenny bit to buy him a few loose woodbines.

*Old man's voice:*

"Why do I feel that one fag on my mantelpiece is an inch shorter than the others because a wee scut treated himself to a few drags from it on his way back from the Widow Flood's?"

*Own voice:*

Was it because I was coughing like an old horse with the heaves or more likely that – even when I was seven – Jamsey saw through me. We were two peas in a pod and Finglas was too small to box either of us in. There's only so much bending in frosty fields any boy can do; slouching home dog-tired at dusk after labouring for the Butterlys of Newpark Farm or the Craigies of Harristown or the Kettles out beyond Cold Winters. No townland ever deserved its name better then Cold Winters. Only a fifteen minute walk from the constabulary barracks, yet Cold Winters would still be thick with hoarfrost when there was soft dew on every other farm from Watery Lane to Slutsend.

*Old man's voice:*

"Your problem, John Bell, is that you have wanderlust worse than mine," Jamsey once said. "But if you do travel, then keep one eye open for danger. When danger appears, like a bullet with your name carved into it, then run for the hills or the sea, but dodge the hell out of its path."

*Own voice:*

Jamsey cadged his way out of Dublin port as a cabin boy; preferring life at sea to labouring in Ballygall and Ballyboggan and Cardiffsbridge and Cardiffscastle for farmers who pay a pittance and keep calling you a boy until you're seventy years old, when they tell you to hobble off home and starve because you're now too ancient to stoop in their fields anymore. He knew seasickness and tiny maggots in the meat during long voyages and scurvy and sunsets over Buenos Aires and women – you knew they were surely beautiful women because Jamsey would go suddenly quiet when reminiscing. His silence contained secrets, because he'd smile to himself and I'd know that he'd want me to leave him alone with his thoughts when he'd say.

*Old man's voice with gruff affection:*

"You've smoked one half of that fag on my mantelpiece, so away with you and smoke the rest of it somewhere where your mother can't see. Half a dollar says you'll do a runner out of his place one day like I did. But don't run off to sea – when you do your exploring make sure there's dry land under your boots."

*Own voice:*

I thought I was taking Jamsey's advice when I donned this army uniform, but there's shag all dry land over here in France. The tramp of a thousand boots will render any meadow to muck and a thousand boots would make for a quiet day in these parts. It's odd though, how quiet days in this war can be the scariest. Maybe because when all hell breaks loose, with shells causing enough racket to waken the dead, you've barely time to think. You're caught up in trying to survive and, if you as much as pause for breath then a toff with a cane and a wax moustache roars dog's abuse at you for being an Irish shirker.

I've seen lads shot, standing feet away from me. Their look of surprise because here in France death seeks out men by random fluke. You don't see the bullet coming until it splatters you to pieces. War is meant to be about King and Kaiser and Home Rule and poor little Catholic Belgium, but a week in the trenches puts paid to such gobbledygook. Maybe toffs still believe in that waffle, or are too cowardly to admit to themselves that such mush is only cow scutter. Still the young toffs are often first out of the trenches, with their dog whistles and canes and little pistols and acne, as if expecting the Hun machine gunners to tug their forelocks, like we used to do whenever the Craigie family drove their horse and cart through Finglas village for their Evensong service in the Protestant Church.

But because Hun machine gunners never learnt servility, they make mincemeat of those toffs, leaving the rest of us poor sods blundering around in No Man's Land with nobody left alive having a bull's notion about what we're meant to be doing out there. You just keep running, hoping to hear someone with a posh accent shout retreat, because if you get separated from your unit, amid the muck and barbed wire and half-dead men begging you to end their misery … well, that's called desertion and the army has a special cure for it, especially if you're Irish – a firing squad.

I've seen men over here missing half their heads but isn't it funny how nothing has ever shocked me more than the first man I saw being shot. Because that wasn't over here in France: it was outside the Widow Flood's pub on the Main Street of Finglas village.

The autumn of 1913 is eighteen months ago but it feels like another life. I was barely more than a boy when Big Jim Larkin, the union leader, stomped out from Dublin city to rile up half the young men of Finglas so that we started spouting sedition and revolution. Or, to be precise, we shouted that we'd slave no more for local farmers till we got paid 17 shillings for a six-day week, with an hour free to rest our limbs and eat a bit of grub during each twelve-hour working day.

In Dublin city Larkin had got the tram drivers out on strike but in Finglas it was us lads that got ourselves out, egging each other on because there's fierce bravery in numbers. And we imagined there was safety in numbers too. We grew so brave that when Butterly's farm workers were too scared to join us, we destroyed a field of Butterly's cabbages and threw their tools in the drain. This new sense of power made us as giddy as March hares: young lads, not used to free time, congregating on the main street, angry after hearing that Kettle's farm were recruiting scabs to bring in their harvest. We were like dry kindling only needing a match. That spark came when some lads shouted that one of Craigie's workers who wouldn't join the strike was supping porter in the Widow Flood's.

I'm not saying that we weren't out of order, with windows broken and name calling. But we were young bucks, dizzy at not knowing how to handle the illusion that, if we stood united, we had some class of power. The two RIC men stationed in the Finglas constabulary barracks didn't know how to handle us either. The bloody fools made things worse by deciding to arm themselves before they timidly poked their heads out of the barracks door. The sight of this only made us grow braver, hurtling a few stones at them from a safe distance. What real harm was in that? No peeler ever died from a pebble bouncing off his helmet. It was ructions and rumpus and rúla búla but no more riotous than back in the old days, when the Humours of Finglas used to be in full flow and they say that any man back then not swinging a blackthorn stick on the main street of Finglas was a proselyting English preacher offering weak soup and eternal damnation.

A few harmless stones may have come within a hair's breadth of Constable Berry but that was no cause for him to kneel and fire four rifle shots at us like we were marauding Zulus. By the third shot most young lads who'd been spouting revolution five minutes earlier had scattered for the North Road, sprinting towards Ashbourne quicker than greyhounds.

I'd have outrun them all, having no personal liking for danger, but I lost my head altogether when I saw young Patrick Daly holding his stomach and stumbling to the ground. I used to knock around with Patrick, robbing orchards and eyeing girls who pretended not to be eyeing us back. A fury overtook me and I shouted at Constable Barry that he'd no need to be shooting us and Constable Barry – looking scared, like he couldn't believe what he'd just done – shouted back that I was a lying blaggard and he'd only been firing blanks.

He shut up though when I showed him the gaping hole in Patrick's stomach and another in his back where the bullet came clean out. The two peelers hoisted Patrick up and dragged him off to Farnham's Madhouse for incurable gentlefolk to see if a doctor might be lodging there, but they glaring back at me to warn me to forget whatever I thought I'd seen or they'd deal with me in their own way too.

Old Jamsey always told me that if you see danger with your name on it, you run. That night in Finglas I saw how any man wearing a uniform can get away with shooting anyone they please and it suddenly struck me that surely the safest place to hide would be behind a uniform myself. How was I to know that a blasted war with Germany would break out ten months later? I just knew that if the Kettle family employed scab labour, it wouldn't be long before other farms did likewise. Winter was coming. My parents had enough mouths to feed without their eldest son being blacklisted by every farmer in ten parishes. There would be little work for any lad marked down as a troublemaker and no work at all for any lad called as a witness in any court case involving the peelers.

I only felt safe when I reached the Royal Barracks opposite Kingsbridge Station up in Dublin and saw well-fed lads my own age square bashing away in peace. There's safety in numbers, I thought again. When the recruiting sergeant asked if I could drive a vehicle, I winked and said there was no vehicle I couldn't drive, provided he found someone patient enough to knock the knack of driving it into my skull. The sergeant winked back and chortled.

*Rough voice:*

"I like a good laugh, John Bell," he said. "And I'll have a right good laugh knocking seven shades of shite out of you if you ever wink at a superior officer again, you bogman from a village so full of scoundrels that you stole St Patrick's goat from him when that saintly man went out to try and convert the heathens of Finglas."

*His own voice as he looks around. His pose has straightened, suggesting a man tied to a post.*

One time I asked Jamsey if he could tie a noose. He laughed and said, "I pray to God, young Bell, that's one knot you'll never get to see." Isn't it funny how God listened to Jamsey's prayer but never listened to mine? Jamsey often called me a rogue but only in affection, because I've never harmed a man or stole from one – beyond the few spuds any labourer might slip into his pocket when leaving a field at dusk, his arms blue with cold.

They say we each have a guardian angel with us, night and day. Growing up in Finglas I'd a name for mine: hunger. In winter hunger taught me how to forage for food, because I was the eldest, with hungrier mouths than mine at home. Besides, I liked being off on my own, setting snares for rabbits or finding clusters of late berries to ease a famished stomach.

Give me an acre of woodland and I'll gather you a feast fit for a king, or for a king too famished to be choosy. That's what I was trying to do, a few months back when my unit were on a trudging march through the scarred French countryside. When the officer told us to fall out and rest near a copse of tress, we'd nothing to look forward to except a gypsy's breakfast: a cigarette, a piss and a good look around.

An English lad named Wilkinson complained about being hungry and so I asked permission to show him how to forage for food because, although half the landscape was destroyed by bomb craters, the untouched parts looked the same as the woods and fields I'd grown up in. Wilkinson and I filled our bellies and then we filled our pockets and hard hats with eatables to bring back as treats for the other chaps. We heard the toff officer shout in at us to hurry but we risked another five minutes because we thought that all we'd get would be a good rollicking and that the other chaps would be amazed at the amount of food we'd bring out.

The secret with toffs is knowing how far to push them. I figured that only a gobdaw would march off and leave two men behind him. But the problem with army toffs is that they're not like the Craigies in Finglas who'd give you a bollicking and let bygones be bygones. As Wilkinson – who is English himself – tried to warn me, English toffs are an entire separate breed of toffs, with ramrods so far up their arses that they can tickle their own tonsils with them.

When we emerged from the woods, our unit had matched off with no sight or sound of them in that half-flattened landscape. Mother of Jesus, we knew we were in trouble, but we just didn't know how much trouble. It shouldn't be hard to find two hundred soldiers marching in formation, but it is when the only things moving for miles are lines of soldiers scurrying like rats with no time to answer questions shouted by two dawdlers running about with hard hats filled with berries.

We spent that night in a French billet and next morning found the makeshift HQ of the 1st Division, where we waited for hours to see an officer, only to finally be told that all officers were too busy to see riff-raff like us. We then cadged our way onto a train crammed with French troops, hoping this might take us in the same direction our unit had gone. We were hours into our journey before Wilkinson overheard the only word of French he understood – Paree – and wherever our unit was matching to towards it sure wasn't Paris. We clambered off in darkness at the next stop. I knew what it was like to run across a No Man's Land of barbed wire and severed limbs, but this new No Man's Land was just as dangerous because by now we knew we were marked down as deserters. It was hard to seek directions from locals with no English and scary to seek directions from officers on horseback who'd want to know what the hell we were doing wandering about on our own. All we could do was frantically search for some person or landmark we recognised and knock on isolated doors to seek food and a floor to sleep on until one morning came when two Gendarmes caught up with us.

Feeling their steel handcuffs cut into my wrists I wished to God that I stayed in Finglas: Constable Barry's threats didn't seem so scary anymore. Still life didn't seem all black when they handed us over to the military authorities. The kindly warder whom Wilkinson greeted assured us that we'd be grand as he locked us in a cell.

*Rural English accent:*

"Soldiers here are always getting separated from their regiments. A rap on the knuckles is all you'll get. The army needs all the men it can lay hands on. It's only Irish lads they shoot, because they need to make examples to stiffen the backbone of the other lazy lice-ridden Paddies."

*Own voice:*

I kept my mouth shut and let Wilkinson talk. Weak tea is bad enough without fearing that the warder might have spat in it when he realised I was Irish. I was saying nothing but thinking fast. This wasn't Kettle's farm where you could do a runner and find another farmer willing to let you slave from him. Or a port where Jamsey said that you could always jump ship and find a sea captain willing to ask no questions, provided you worked your passage for free. I knew damn all about life but I knew enough to know that I stood a fair chance of being stood against a wall and shot unless I got out of that military prison. If I could find my way back to my own battalion then surely to God they couldn't call me a shirker, because my own captain knew that, while I might be a Jack-the-lad at times, there's no real harm in me. And if I managed to stumble upon a French seaport instead then I'd take my chances of hopefully not being found as a stowaway when the ship docked in Southampton, because England must surely be a big enough place to swallow up any man, if nobody came looking too hard for him.

Christmas day arrived – the Christmas the toffs had promised us that this war would be over by. By now I knew it wasn't my war and that this war won't be over any Christmastime soon. On St Stephen's night, with the warders drunk, I saw my chance to leave Wilkinson and flee. I'd no idea where I was going, racing through pitch dark French countryside but I wasn't thinking straight anymore. Fear does something to your brain. It's one thing to stumble through No Man's Land, not knowing where the bullet will come from. But it's another thing to know that the bullets will come from ten paces, fired by young buck-eejits so scared they'd probably make such a dog's dinner of my execution, with some toff needing to finish me off with his revolver pressed to my skull.

That same St Stephen's night the Finglas lads were surely having the right crack, hunting the wren. I should have been out with the Luby and Emmett and Flood lads, making mischief and music as we landed in on farmhouses as far off as St Margaret's and saved our last call for the McCourts near Dubber Cross where old man McCourt always poured a generous measure for any visitor.

Instead I was on my own; scared witless and clueless, knowing that, for all my running, I had as much chance of escaping as a pig trapped in a pen when a farmer is sharpening the knife for his throat. I kept wanting to pretend that I was racing up through the great oaks in Finglas Wood, past Farnham's asylum, knowing that the main street was about to rise up before me, with its pubs and shops nestling around the church. I had as much chance of finding Timbuktu as reaching Finglas but during those three desperate weeks, when I foraged where I could and slept in ditches, I wasn't thinking straight anymore. My dreams were filled with horrors I'd seen in the trenches and when I woke all I could smell was my own fear. I remember thinking how vast France was, with farmhouses ruined and squadrons of men on every road, led by suspicious officers who turned their heads whenever they spied me.

I kept my head down as if pretending that I knew where I was going, surviving on berries and apples from an orchard I stumbled across, with half the trees bombed to smithereens. Nothing keeps you moving like fear: fear the Germans would blast me to kingdom come if I found my own battalion or that a court-martial would hasten my death if I didn't. I don't know what I was thinking, because what does a terrified dog think about when running away from a beating, except to keep running. Still no matter how far you run, you'll eventually run into someone – and I did: the Assistant Provost-Marshal at Saint-Omer, with more wax in his moustache that in an entire altar of candles.

*Posh English accent:*

"You there, who do you belong to?"

*Own voice:*

I sure as hell didn't belong there, I should have told him: I'd only joined your blasted army to dodge the peelers in Finglas. But there was no point telling him anything, least of all the story of how a soldier can just slack off for a few minutes to forage for berries in a wood and find his world turned upside-down. I now had a reputation for myself, having gone missing twice. Their sole regret during my court martial was that they could only shoot me once.

You'd have thought that I wouldn't get a wink of sleep last night: it being my last night on earth. But a hard bunk feels like a soft bunk after weeks of sleeping in ditches. I had vivid dreams of Finglas and of my sisters, Kate and Anne and Sara and Theresa and little James who's only four but today will suddenly become the man in the family. He'll be too young to even remember his big brother: John Bell of Finglas, aged twenty when shot. I'm thinking now wasn't I the right fool to have not paid to have at least one photograph of me taken in my uniform. I'm wondering what day of the week this is too, because my mother draws my wages from the Post Office in Finglas every Wednesday. A driver only earns one shilling and five ha'pennies a day but, if they are slow with their forms, maybe she'll get one last week's pay out of me.

The post mistress will know I'm dead when my wages stop and, once that gossip-monger knows, then all of Finglas will know. But they won't really understand anything because half of them have never travelled as far as Howth. How could they know what it feels like to see a man have his face half blown off and yet still alive for a whole minute in a trench beside you? Or if not still alive, then at least still staggering about, like a chicken with its head chopped off.

I say one thing. Dawn comes fierce early in France. Sheep will be lambing now on Craigie's farm; men tramping out from Finglas village to Cold Winters and Ballygall, Woodbine smoke in the still air. The officer who knocked on my cell door ten minutes ago was respectful enough. "It's time," he said. I could smell new grass trying to break through the mud they marched me across, with the firing party having little to say and me saying even less. The questions that should be bothering me are just too enormous to ask, with this palatable terror in my heart. Eternity? Heaven? Oblivion? I wish I'd paid more attention in class and church, but maybe secretly in their hearts teachers and priests know as little about what comes next as the rest of us? Or in my case, what comes after what comes next. Because I know what comes next. At whatever second is officially deemed to be dawn, a toff will issue a command to these six poor blighters who look as scared as myself.

I'm stood upright here – no slouching allowed. My feet are neatly tied, exactly twelve inches apart. My hands are tied behind my back, with six inches of rope left loose between my bound wrists and the wooden post. It's a special knot they use, the guard in my cell confided to me last night. The war office in London provide a diagram to ensure that no unsightly burn marks scar my wrists after the firing squad do their work and bury my corpse immediately afterwards.

All I can think about now is to wonder why the hell I didn't ask the guard in my cell for the name of the blasted rope knot they're using on my hands so I can tell Jamsey if our paths ever cross in whatever version of hell or paradise I'll wake up in. Jamsey will be the first person on our lane to know I'm dead because he can recognise every footstep. Few letters come for anyone on our lane and no telegrams. He'll know from the light footstep that a boy is approaching and from his hesitant walk that it's the telegram boy bringing bad news.

Those whose sons get shot in the trenches receive long letters from chaplains and officers full of comforting lies … "A brave soldier … a quick death … your son had no time to feel any pain". They never write about the days and nights some lads spend crying out and then whimpering before they die, impaled on barbed wire. But few families will get a communiqué as short as the one that will be tapped across the telegraph wires to reach Finglas tomorrow. My father will be too unworldly to fully grasp what those three short sentences mean. He'll read them aloud to Jamsey, asking what did I do; why are these the only words that history will remember me for? "Driver John Bell of Finglas, Dublin. Royal Field Artillery. Shot at dawn."

*Lights down. Blackout.*

# Waiting to be Found

*Waiting To be Found* was first performed, in abridged form, on the stage of the Abbey Theatre, Dublin, on 22 February 2017 as part of the Dublin's Culture Connects: The National Neighbourhood Press Play Showcase. It was first performed in its entirety, by the same actress, in an open air performance in St Canice's graveyard in Finglas – the small graveyard where the play is set – on Saturday, 25 February 2017.

Performer:     Ali Dempsey
Director:      Elizabeth Duffy

*In memory of Thomas (Dano) Lynch of Barrack Lane, Finglas, Dublin; caretaker of St Canice's Cemetery, Finglas who generously made visitors welcome there – including the author as a teenager – for many decades, and who passed away in April, 2017, two months after this play received its first full performance in the small graveyard which he so carefully tended.*

*Lights come up on KELLIE, a seventeen-year-old girl, who, in real time in this play, is leaning against the ancient Nether Cross, located in the small but relatively unnoticed graveyard close to the busy dual carriageway which slices through the old centre of Finglas village – a working class suburb of North Dublin. However there is no necessity for the set design to overtly recreate the specifics of this actual setting and so a director or stage designer may choose to dress the stage with a set as minimal as just a cross or box or any other structure for the performer to sit on at times. KELLIE looks up and addresses the audience.*

KELLIE: You always have to get the key to this graveyard by knocking at the caretaker's cottage door on Barracks Lane, just before the gate here on Wellmount Road. His family don't mind, like, they're friendly and helpful, but, all the same, it's a family's door you're knocking on and so you feel … or at least, well, I feel … a bit embarrassed if I wander down here too often to ask them for the key to open up these ancient rusty iron gates.

Because, I mean, it's not as if I have anyone belonging to me buried in this tiny ancient graveyard that feels like such an oasis of calm, cut off on one side by the dual carriageway and by ugly new apartment blocks on the other. In fact I don't even know anybody who has a relation buried in here. It's hard to believe that some people living here in Finglas still have roots that stretch back this far. But there must be some of the old Finglas families left because once or twice I've seen these graveyard gates standing open to allow a coffin and a small band of mourners to troop in here.

It's funny to think that, scattered amid all the estates crammed with thousands of people like me who just happen to be born here, some families' roots go right back to when Finglas was just a village. But the only difference now between them and all the rest of us is that they still have family plots in this cemetery or burial rights or whatever legal phrase they use.

I bet you it's some snazzy official term; a phrase that I'd just need to repeat once and nobody would ever again question what I'm doing standing here alone like an eejit, surrounded by slanted and collapsed slabs of tombstones, with chiselled lettering so faded that you'd swear they'd been written in raindrops by a child's finger.

To be honest, I know feck all about those barely legible names of these tombstones. I don't visit this locked graveyard to feel closer to the dead. I know this sounds stupid, and I'd never tell anyone else, but I come here to feel closer to someone who's missing and – in an odd sort of way – I come here to feel closer to myself.

I don't mean to feel closer to the person that I am now, because half the time I barely know who I am these days. I'm a seventeen-year-old cocktail of self-doubt and self-contradiction and at times self-loathing. At other times I'm filled with mad, delirious happiness and brim-full of pent-up longings and dreams and love that I haven't got the words to express yet, and with passionate desire … oh yes … red hot sparks of sexual desire that fizzle up inside me at the oddest moments when I look across the classroom at a boy whose brains don't match his biceps and who hasn't enough cop on to turn his head and notice my glazed-over look that has every other girl in the class nudging each other and laughing. Not that I'd want to be any of those girls, because, to be honest, while I know shag all about almost everything in life, this still means that I know twice as much as most other girls in my class.

I know it because I've needed to grow up quick. Some girls in my class think that being grown up involves sending texts to their boyfriends at midnight in the hopes of driving him so crazy with lust he won't be able to sleep. Then they wind up unable to sleep themselves, terrified that he'll forward their photos and texts on to his mates. I think they're addicted – not to risk or romance or love, but to the giddy whirl of attention; to being the girl at the centre of a scrum of other girls peering at her phone. The giddy whirl of being fancied by a boy or letting a boy know that they fancy him; the whirl of "will he or won't he?", then the first date and the giddy post-mortem dissection of it with their pals and the standard post-mortem over every word and touch that occurs during the all-important second date. By the third date it's stale news, isn't it, champagne bubbles gone flat. The only way to get back that giddiness is to break up with the boy, just for the adrenalin rush of being at the centre of renewed attention; the warm weather front of public sympathy moving in from the Azores, with her pals wondering how long more they need to keep calling the boy a louse before they make a move to snaffle him up for themselves.

That's part of growing up and secretly one part of me wishes that I could play those games too. But that's not actually being grown up. Being grown up is different. I can't tell you exactly how different because in reality I haven't really done too much living yet. But I think that the feel of being grown up starts with a chill that lodges in your bones when you wake up one morning to find that someone you love is gone and that – deep down inside where no one else can see … you suddenly feel ten years older than when you fell asleep the previous night.

The teachers who write school reports about me in neat red biro don't seem to have a clue about who I actually am or what I feel any more. Maybe that's good, because maybe when I was younger I was far too much of an open book. Too innocent. Innocence is a feeling I miss. But that's enough about who I am now, because this *me* – the *me* you're looking at – she isn't the *me* that I visit this graveyard to be with. I come here to feel close to two other versions of myself – the child that I once was and the young woman whom I don't really know yet but that I feel sure I will one day become.

My Da used to bring me here before Da went missing. Maybe missing isn't the right word, but he's certainly missing from my life. I like how the word *missing* covers a multitude of things. A doctor looking up from test results to say "you have a malign condition that unfortunately is incompatible with life". Or what happens to a man pressurised into hiding money or drugs or guns for hard chaws who don't take kindly to the cops stumbling across them. Of course you don't really go missing in that case – you go into a state of being unfound until a few hillwalkers stumble across your corpse months later with your hands bound. Or maybe the person who goes missing was missing something within his own life – missing how he used to be able to look into his partner's eyes and see love for him reflected back in her gaze. Maybe when love goes missing, you go missing in search of it too. You go searching for yourself in vodka or by slipping off to Glasgow where any man in the Celtic shirt will seamlessly blend into at last one half of that city I've never been in.

Or maybe you simply miss the last bus home and think, sure I'll walk home to Finglas like I did a hundred times when I was younger – why waste a taxi fare when I'm saving up to buy my daughter something for her birthday. But maybe a junkie lurking with a knife in Phibsborough doesn't miss you and your wallet that he's after or maybe a scared elderly man, driving his wife into the 24 hour Accident and Emergency ward in the Mater Hospital, ploughs straight into you when he loses control and mounts the footpath, distracted by his wife's cries of distress.

Maybe it's something as ordinary as a heart attack on a soccer pitch or maybe nobody ever knows exactly what caused someone else to go missing. All I'm willing to say to you is that Da will never be dead to me, though when I look at the lines on my mother's face – as if a crow had pressed its webbed feet against her eyes – I know that my da is surely dead for her. But even still his absence is ever present in her long silences and on the nights when I come downstairs to find her chain-smoking in the kitchen, whereas at one time not even George Clooney would have been allowed to light up under her roof, unless possibly after sex and only then if he washed up the dishes afterwards.

Ma hated the smell of cigarette smoke and she hated the smell of Da's sweat too when he'd come home on Saturday afternoons, after playing soccer on the muddy pitches off Kildonan Avenue. His burly macho teammates all needed bigger bags to hold their L'Oréal revitalising sports body washes and Mancave Cedarwood Shower gels than the bags they needed for their football gear. But all Da ever did was just throw on a pair of jeans and a T-shirt and sling his boots over his shoulder after every match, because he didn't like me hanging around outside the changing rooms where he thought that I might hear language a girl shouldn't hear.

Or maybe he didn't want to cut into that special time we shared together after those football matches. I never missed a home match that he played in. Off we'd go together after the final whistle, discussing the game because while I was a daddy's girl, I was also a tomboy who understood the vagaries of the offside rule. But we didn't just talk about soccer: we'd talk about school or about anything … or at least anything but Ma. And on most of those Saturday afternoons, if it wasn't raining when we passed the locked gates of this cemetery he'd say, "Sure I'll give old Mr Lynch, the caretaker, a knock and see if he has the key handy."

I'd nod casually but inside I'd be giddy with excitement because once this old gate creaked open with a low groan, as if reluctant to let us step into the past here, something subtly changed between us. Now don't get me wrong. This graveyard was our secret but there was nothing secretive about what we did or said in here, nothing that we couldn't have told to anyone else. But we never did tell anyone about the snatched fifteen minute spells when we lingered here, because this was our special time, stolen from time, when we spoke differently, when Da made me feel … well, not actually grown up … but when Da's conversation held out the promise that one day I'd become truly special when I did grow up and discovered who I truly am … because Da always claimed I had a special gift inside me just waiting to be unearthed.

Unearthed seems an odd word, though perhaps not so much in a graveyard. But it's the word that I use because of the story he told me on the first afternoon he brought me here. The same story I made him tell every time we came here – getting annoyed if he left out or changed a single word – because, for that story to retain its magic, it had to always be told in the exact same way he'd first told me, back when I was old enough to understand it on one level, but still too young to grasp the point that he was really trying to make.

That's the odd thing about most boys and men – they need to hide their intelligence when together in a group, bury it behind banter and crude jokes. Only when they're alone with you do they feel truly able to be themselves. Da might have become a professor of history in some university if he hadn't been born in Finglas. No, that's not true – Finglas has produced its share of professors and doctors and scientists and whatnot. Da's curse, back when he was at my age, was that his true talent – having the gift of an inquisitive mind – hadn't been unearthed yet and his other talent – the talent that everyone else had been obsessed with since he was nine years old – just wasn't strong enough in the end.

Nobody ever stands on the side of a football pitch looking for someone with a brilliant brain, but when Da was a teenager scouts for big English clubs were always turning up at Corporation pitches in the hopes of unearthing a gangly striker who might earn them a trickledown kickback commission if the lad made the grade amid the herds of other boys lured into leaving their schooling and their family and friends behind by signing schoolboy forms with football clubs who would later ditch 95% of them the day they turned eighteen years of age.

Da was unearthed by a scout, playing for Tolka Rovers at fifteen. By eighteen he was a veteran – after three years of homesickness in London; three years of cleaning the boots of famous first team players; three years of being a local legend back in Finglas, being talked about in awe by his mates until his mates simply grew bored by the injures hampering his progress and got on with their own lives and their Leaving Certs. At eighteen Da was dumped by that big business English football club: sent home with a couple of signed jerseys and his tail between his legs. Everyone in Finglas knew what Da was by then – a failure. Oh, he could have played League of Ireland or at least played at a far higher level than a local Finglas street team but, after he came home, Da not only had a living to make as a factory hand, but he also had a life to catch up on, away from training sessions and broken metatarsal bones that had left him side-lined for months and haplessly trying to play catch up in pursuit of those professional contracts for tantalisingly huge wages that were always tantalisingly just out of his reach.

Da was twenty-four before he put his sense of failure behind him and realised that this soccer star whom everyone had wanted him to be was never the person whom he actually was inside. It took him until then to unearth in his own mind who he was truly was and realise that his true vocation – if his life hadn't been hijacked – would have been to be a teacher. By then he was already married and with me on the way. He'd made a life for himself back here in Finglas before discovering that the limits of his life didn't actually fit his inner self. But it was too late to talk about enrolling in college as a mature student when he was a married man about to take on the responsibilities of being a father.

Not that he ever really talked about this or complained in any way about his life. But I knew that he would have made a great teacher because he was passionate about explaining things and making complex ideas simple. On that first occasion when he told me the story of this cross I thought was he was just being passionate about the past too. But the past wasn't actually what he was trying to tell me about, although he could make it come alive. He'd stand over there inside the crumbling ruined church in this graveyard and, just by waving his hands, he could transform that derelict space into a medieval nave and chancel and a side aisle which he said was once used as a school. He'd describe how a church on this spot had survived the onslaught of the Vikings and was still in use when Cromwell arrived in Ireland in 1648, acting like the ultimate English football hooligan and determined to smash every Catholic relic he encountered.

Cromwell's troops were meant to march through Finglas on his way north to slaughter the entire population of Drogheda to teach them to be good loyal subjects ever after. Like many an English football hooligan his sense of direction wasn't great and he went a different route in the end. But the local Finglas families weren't willing to take the risk that he might destroy this ancient cross if he and his thuggish ultras marched back this way after their rampages and slaughter in Drogheda. This cross was the last precious reminder which people had of the great monastery which had once stood here, back when

Finglas was such a famous seat of learning that Da would have fitted right in. So those local families gathered under cover of darkness to secretly dismantle the cross and bury it in the glebe field, so that it would lie there, unmarked and hidden from the hooves of invading armies, its location kept as a secret locked away in people's hearts.

I keep a lot locked away in my heart these days: secrets I've told no one about because my dreams are still only half-formed. That's what Da was trying to tell me before he went missing – that sometimes you need to keep your dreams buried away until the time is right to bring them out into the light. I'm doing my Leaving Cert exams in a few months' time, and why is it that, all of a sudden, everyone seems to expect me to know who it is that I am and what it is that I want to be; as if understanding my future should be as simple as me filling in a wish-list of college courses on the Central Applications Office form? Do I know what I want? No. Do I ever know who I am? All I know is that there's a hidden invisible pearl deep inside me. Pearls are created out of pain, out of grains of sand that turn into grit that get painfully lodged inside an oyster shell and it's only when the oyster shell is finally prised open that the beauty of the pearl is revealed.

Da didn't have a clue who he really was at fifteen years of age when those talent scouts came calling, thinking they had unearthed his true talent. He still didn't know at eighteen when he got offloaded by that club, or at twenty-four when he first held me in his arms. Maybe he was still trying to figure out just exactly who he was on the day when he went missing from our lives. But Da knew that you need to keep on probing deeper and deeper into the bedrock inside you until you finally unearth your secret. Most girls in my class say that I'm as odd as two left socks, but do I honestly give a curse about their snide tweets or their bullying on Facebook? It's their own vulnerability that makes that cling together in packs – anxious to display the same clothes, the same labels on their trainers, paralysed by a desperate fear that anyone might think them odd or different.

I am odd and I am different. My heart brims with emotions and thoughts that I lack the words to express yet. But that's OK. This is what Da kept trying to tell me whenever he'd talk about this cross. That sometimes you need to bury your treasure away, so deeply and for so long inside you that you fear nobody will ever unearth it.

When Da talked to me about the Nether Cross he didn't just conjure up Finglas two hundred years ago: he summoned up St. Petersburg and Constantinople and Rio de Janeiro – all the places that a Protestant clergyman named Robert Walsh, who'd been a friend of Robert Emmet's, travelled to before he came back here to Finglas to die. Walsh had a passion for unearthing secrets. He once travelled through the dangerous jungles of Brazil to unearth the truth about the wretched conditions slaves were kept in, so that he could campaign for the abolition of slavery.

But long before he unearthed those dark secrets in Brazil he stood in this small graveyard in 1816 after being posted here as a curate. He'd heard a whisper, or maybe he just had a second sense, that a secret had been buried here since 1649. A secret which seemed lost after a hundred and sixty-seven years but which was never truly forgotten because it was quietly passed from generation to generation among the old Finglas families.

Da enjoyed acting out the parts when telling his story. The role of the eager young clergyman fascinated by rumours of an ancient cross and the role of the oldest man in the village, the sole guardian who had kept this secret alive: a man so ancient that he'd lost track of his own age and barely knew what day of the week it was. But this old man knew – having been sworn to secrecy when told by his dying grandfather, who had been sworn to secrecy by his grandfather in turn, that this cross had secretly been buried in Finglas for safe keeping. He kept this treasure safe until he felt the time was right. Now – with what final strength he could summon – he stood at the exact spot and told the young clergyman: "this is the place and now is the hour."

Da used to make a noise like the sound of spades slicing away through the soft earth and then suddenly striking stone. He'd pretend to be the young curate excitedly clambering down into the hole to let his fingers peel away the sackcloth so that he could touch stone carvings crafted here by monks a thousand years ago. Reverend Walsh may have later gone off to battle slave traders in Brazil, but before he did so he erected this cross again on this spot where it could become an everyday mystery, a marvel that had lain hidden for almost seventeen decades and which has now stood on this spot for two centuries, with Finglas so busy chopping and changing around it and people so frantically getting on with their lives that nobody has time to stop and consider the wonder of how this pearl was unearthed.

Da sometimes laughed at the end of his story and said that, just because nobody can see how a thing is truly wondrous, doesn't mean that the wonder doesn't exist. Today this cross is hidden in full view, with nobody speeding past in their cars having time to understand its story. But Da told it to me and I'll telling it to you. I'm clinging to the truth inside his story because now I no longer have him to cling to; now I'm learning to grow up fast in a house filled with my mother's cigarette smoke and silence.

I don't know what secret Da glimpsed buried away inside me when he used to look at me and smile on the afternoons we lingered here. But I know that he saw some hidden talent I can still only guess at because it's not ready to be unearthed yet. So what I'm just trying to tell you now is what I think he was trying to tell me; that it's perfectly all right that I don't have a clue about who I am yet. I just need to stay true to myself, even if I haven't any sense of who I will become. Da kept trying to explain that life isn't about knowing all the answers, it's about learning how to listen out for clues. It's about knowing how this pain that I'm feeling now is the grit and sand which needs to be lodged inside of me so that one day, when I'm ready to open up the shell of myself, I'll discover whatever luminous pearl is glistening inside me.

On some nights I think the sounds of the shovels trying to reach me are so far away that they'll never find me and on other nights I hear them so close that they sound only inches away. But what do I know when, like I say, I'm just a seventeen-year-old cocktail of contradictions and self-doubt and passers-by are probably sniggering now at the sight of me sitting alone here beside this cross, like I've been stood up on a date. Let strangers stare because I don't care. I just know that invisible shovels are whirling through the air above my head and one day they'll strike against stone and I'll tear aside the faded sackcloth. That's when I'll see what Da kept hinting at: the secret of who I truly am finally revealed. I'll see myself reflected back in a smooth pearl and I will recognise – and remain true to – the woman I'm destined to become.

*Lights go down*